CW01626832

THE A-Z OF

HUMAN PERFORMANCE

Emma Wiggs

Jonna Sercombe

Steve Eaton

CONTENTS

THE AUTHORS

Emma Wiggs

Emma Wiggs is a paralympic gold medalist and eight times paracanoe world champion. Since a mystery virus impaired her mobility in her legs, Emma has fought her way to the top, dedicating herself to the mastery of, not just one, but two sports; at two different paralympic games.

To book Emma for a keynote please contact **ewiggs@hotmail.com**

Steve Eaton

Steve Eaton is a Performance Coach & Consultant working with organisations and individuals that work in the most challenging circumstances, using expertise gained via his own fascinating career. His long standing interests are resilience and potential trauma management.

To book Steve for a keynote or coaching please contact **steve.eaton@panurgypd.com**

Jonna Sercombe

Jonna Sercombe is a cognitive scientist turned marketeer turned entrepreneur who has spent the last 20 years developing leaders in some of the worlds most famous companies. CEO of Interactive Workshops, he has built an intriguing small company with a big impact and authored four books on teams and leadership.

To book Jonna for a keynote or L&D consulting project please contact **jonna@interactiveworkshops.com**

FOREWORD, AND A BIT OF FORETHOUGHT

Thanks for getting hold of our book. People read for all sorts of reasons. Some people skim the pages and stop when their eye is caught. Some like to sit down with a cup of tea and read in one go. Whatever your style, dive in. Enjoy. For context, let me just share a brief story.

I first worked with Steve and Emma running a strategic leadership programme for a very successful global company. The group had tasked me to source real "experts" for their monthly workshops. I tried not to take that personally. Yet it did make me think: Maybe I'm just a generalist. Who can I bring in that really knows their stuff? I forget who I met first, but I do remember both moments clearly. Steve strolled through a wood in Cambridgeshire as the sun set. Around a campfire, he shared his deep knowledge of what it takes to excel in some of the most challenging environments on earth and how mastering certain basic human skills can have a huge affect on performance levels in many other, highly stressful settings. I only later found out about his years of university study on the subject of performing under pressure. I made mental notes. ("The release of cortisol is slowed by movement.") A couple of years later he took me for a long walk along Bournemouth beach to help me straighten out my own mind after a consolidated season of work pressure and an unwanted ECG made me realise that stress was taking its toll on me. I was rejuvenated by his company and his advice.

When Emma rolled into a meeting room at the National Watersports Center in Nottingham I was somewhat taken aback. She actually was squeezing in her keynote between gym sessions. Slightly sweaty, and with an uncanny knack of making us all relax, she regaled us with her lifestory in such a humble and animated style that none of us who were there will ever forget. Her narrative of the challenging episodes in her life and her pure drive to make the most of the talents she has are contagious. We all left the room reciting mantras. "Plan the paddle. Paddle the plan". Some had that turned into wrist bands. Somehow in her life Emma has worked out how to turn everything for good, and leave no stone unturned in her pursuit of her best. Multiple world champion. Paralympic Gold. Paralymic participation in two sports. And that humour. Also, world class.

And then the weird bit. The longer I spent with these two very well thought-through individuals, the more I noticed a pattern. In completely different fields we were all working from the same set of principles. Whether choosing your attitude, sleep, support networks, family, Steve and Emma were living their lives around the same fundamental beliefs, processes and self-talk I had used to build a business, stay healthy whilst flying the world, lead, manage, innovate. And every single one of those principles made life simpler, not more complicated. Interesting. I had the idea that if we could get together and write, we could create something intriguing, helpful and valuable. Maybe it would be nothing new. After all, we each leaned heavily on the wisdom of others. Yet maybe we could share our ideas and stories. Maybe collaboration could output something useful. We wrote this book together in the year of 2020. We all know what that means. Zoom calls. In a series of writing afternoons we chatted and shared. Then focused for a sprint of writing. We planned our paddle. The A-Z format gave us a framework to capture the key topics. We each took charge of some subjects we love. Then we paddled our plan.

Some of the writing is quite good. And if I could distil the whole book down to one thing it is this.

You can choose.

Whether your attitude, your job, your friends, or even simply how we respond to life's most challenging situations. We can choose. That's also all it takes to achieve your potential. A dedicated life of wise choices, informed by the wisdom of others. As Emma says, "gold medals are not within our control". Neither are company valuations, promotions, even our health. Yet we can choose. We can set out and follow processes that are within our control. Form habits. Build support networks. There are 26 things we can do just in this book. Each improves the possibility that maybe... just maybe... the outcome follows.

We hope you enjoy the thoughts, whether a dip or a deep dive.

Jonna Sercombe
Founder & CEO
Interactive Workshops

A

ATTITUDE AT ALTITUDE

"If you think you can or
think you can't, you're right."

— Henry Ford

To perform well at anything, even under extreme pressure, it's our attitude that ultimately drives our performance. To succeed, we must believe in what we're doing. Whether it's addressing issues regarding life in general, achieving a long-term ambition or succeeding at an elite level, we must ensure that our head and body are in the right place from the outset to give ourselves the very best chance of success. Choosing a positive attitude in life fosters desire and strengthens our beliefs and meaningful sense of purpose. Whereas adopting a negative attitude often leads to disappointment as well as an unpleasant journey along the way. In his highly acclaimed book, Man's Search for Meaning, Viktor Frankl wrote: 'Everything can be taken from a man but one thing: the last of the human freedom to choose one's attitude in any given set of circumstances, to choose one's own way.'

In choosing our attitude to succeed, we are choosing a proactive mindset that works for us: individually, if we're the sole component and collectively, as an attitude that aligns with the other members of an effective team. This pragmatic 'way of addressing something' should be flexible in nature, to adapt to the environment we're in, but it should embody our values and beliefs and reinforce our own distinctive sense of purpose (i.e. your attitude is driven by you.) More accurately, it's driven by your thoughts, your feelings and your behaviour (i.e. the way you think about, feel or do things). These are the only things that we as humans can actually control, so learning to master our attitude is vital in leading a meaningful and fulfilling life. We can often influence certain things around us in society, by how we choose to perceive them and by the way we behave, but as we can't actually control them, we must be able to adapt to them.

As stated, all we can control (with practice) is how (or what) we think, how (or what) we feel and how we act (what we do about it). This is why attitude is the key to unlocking our personal potential or, looking at it another way, creating a solid platform (or foundation) from which to operate. If the foundations of a structure are weak then what's built on top will eventually collapse under pressure. A firm foundation will allow the building above to withstand the pressures and stressors that it's subjected to. Whatever metaphor you choose to use, you should bear in mind that you can have all the skills and knowledge available but without a sound purposeful, robust yet flexible attitude to drive you, or to provide a solid platform from which to operate, you will rarely be as good as you wish to be.

When I reflect on things that I've got right over the years, or things I've achieved, even against the odds, it is often because I've applied a can-do, or want-to-do, attitude. On the flip

Triangle of Success

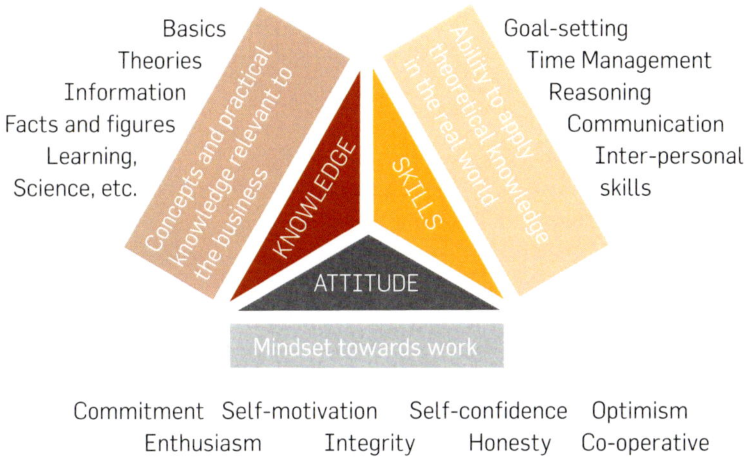

side, when I've got things wrong, and sometimes quite badly wrong, it is often because I've been in a negative frame of mind, and my attitude has been poor or has not been fully engaged. Perhaps I haven't seen the benefits of investing time and effort in committing to something. Maybe I've pushed back against something or someone that I didn't agree with or with whom I felt misaligned for whatever reason and sometimes I've simply got it wrong! Operating with a dismissive or belligerent mindset, however, will almost always thwart elevated levels of performance and will, in most cases, prove self-defeating. So, over the years I've realised that if I want to achieve something that will require personal effort and resources, I firstly need to fully understand why I want to do it. Once I've agreed with myself that it's a good idea, I need to apply a positive mental attitude to the process which involves management of how I think, how I feel and what I do.

However, even the most hardy and upbeat attitudes do not always protect us from losing or falling short of a mark. If only! Having a positive mindset does not mean that we always get things right. It simply means that we understand that, in trying to accomplish something, especially when it's something novel or arduous, we sometimes get it right and sometimes we get it wrong. As humans, we are indeed all fallible. We all make mistakes and we all get things wrong from time to time. Sometimes, however, we are simply not, at that moment perhaps, good enough for the task. The main thing is that we acknowledge that not succeeding at something, however important or trivial, can provide a unique learning experience and an opportunity to develop and grow as a person. Facing adversity can be where our attitude shows it's true colours and is actually needed for building personal resilience. Feeling bad, feeling guilty, sad or angry is fine… for now, because they're just normal human emotions felt as a result of the unpleasant experience. We don't need to like losing or suffering but it's where our attitude has an opportunity to say: 'Hey, wow, I didn't really enjoy that, so what and how can I learn from the experience' and 'What do I need to do to better prepare myself for next time?'

It is often worth acknowledging that in aiming high we often put ourselves in peril of having to live with setbacks. Sometimes, we just need to pick ourselves up, dust ourselves down, process the experience, accept what has happened and move on, hopefully as a richer person for the experience. Having the right flexible attitude, and an optimistic outlook on life, encourages us to maintain an open mind which, in turn, helps us maintain our general awareness, increase our understanding, adapt to our surroundings and manage our personal resilience.

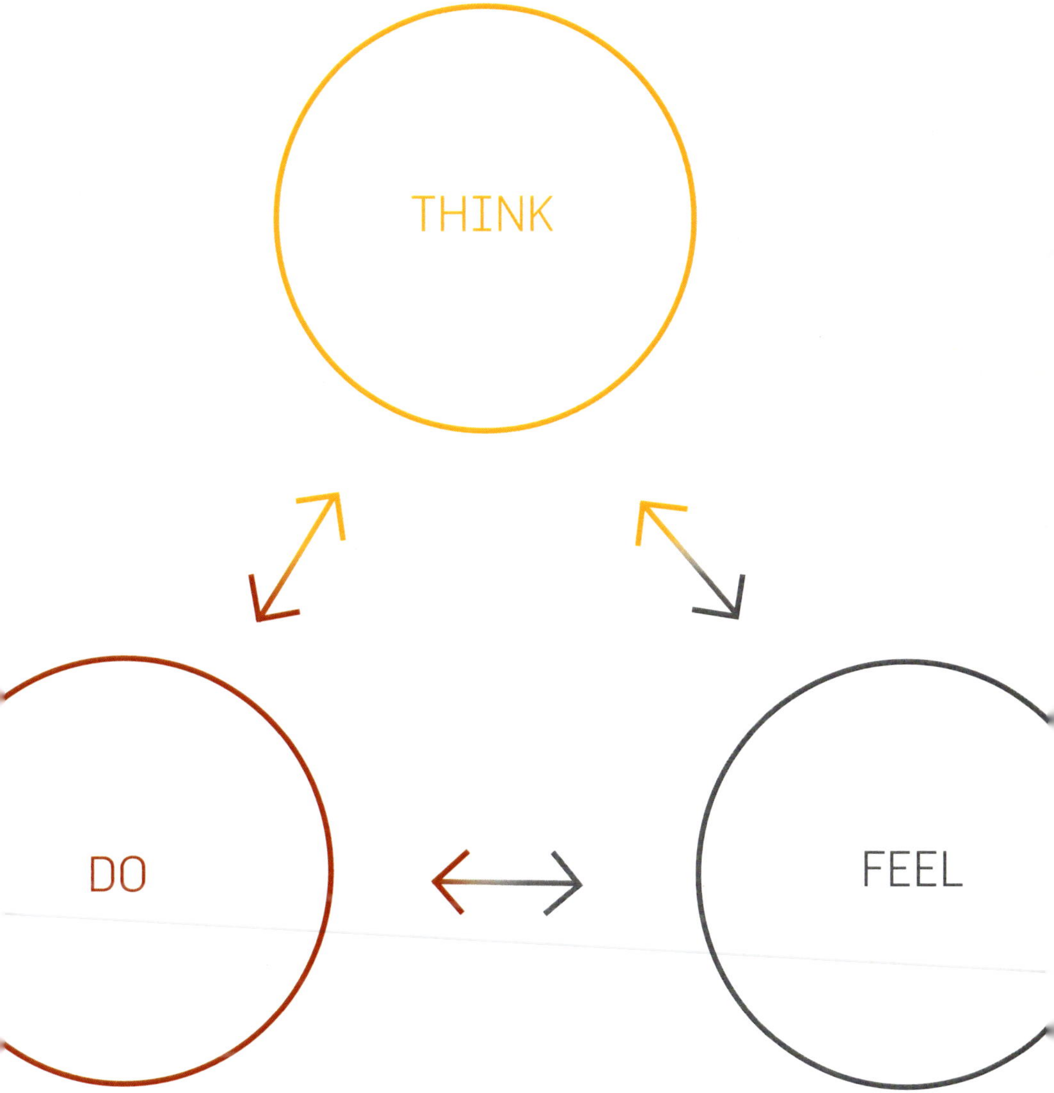
THINK
DO
FEEL

Choosing

Jonna considers learning how to choose our attitude is one of the greatest gifts in life. "My dad used to offer me some pocket money for small jobs when I was young. Things like stacking the woodpile. Mowing the lawn. The pay structure was fascinating. It was £1 for doing the job, and another £1 for doing it with a great attitude. My dad was teaching me a lifelong lesson. Our attitude is as valuable as our output. And we can choose our attitude. I learned that a boss (or paymaster) is willing to pay double for a job done well by a cheerful worker. One of my early bosses was always cheery and super-positive. When I asked him why, he said he chose never to arrive at the office without choosing his attitude. He had a certain roundabout on the journey to work, and he would circle this one extra time as a trigger. From that point on it was all positivity. As Zig Ziglar said: 'It's your attitude, not your aptitude, that will determine your altitude'.

But let's ask a different question.

Can we perform at a high level without learning how to master our attitude? Without control of our attitude we are like a tiny boat; a skiff, or worse, a coracle. When the wind blows, we have no steering. We will be at the mercy of other people and events. We will enter into negative mindsets and moods. We will externalise that and say it's the fault of others. We will waste time, energy, emotion, probably other people's time. It's a vicious cycle.

Mastering a positive attitude in the day-to-day is a fundamental of elite performance. It's a fundamental part of managing our inner dialogues. Imagine attitude is the colour of your words. You might say: 'I can do this.' But if it has no shine, no sparkle, it's perhaps a flat grey. Yet with an intentional attitude the words 'I can do this' might be on fire, burning red-hot with passion.

Choosing our attitude is particularly valuable when it comes to setbacks. Can we learn to choose our attitude when we are suffering, injured? When we have lost money? When we are angry, upset, tired, cold? Or when a business deal has gone wrong, a product failed? When we are being blamed, told we are a bad person, leader, partner, parent? For me, these are the tough moments where I waver between allowing myself to wallow or choosing to live on a higher plane.

Coaching Questions

1. Choose: If you could choose your attitude every day, how would you choose to be? (You might describe feelings or mindsets, think also about posture and energy, or perhaps a colour or animal that works as a metaphor.)

2. Copy: Who can you copy that excels in choosing their attitude?

3. Humble: In maintaining a positive mental attitude try to remain humble, knowing that we can always learn something from any experience (even the most challenging ones) at any age.

4. Rise: In what phase of your life have you most consistently lived as your higher or best self? What was going on that allowed you to rise above?

5. Setbacks: When setbacks happen, what are you going to say to yourself?

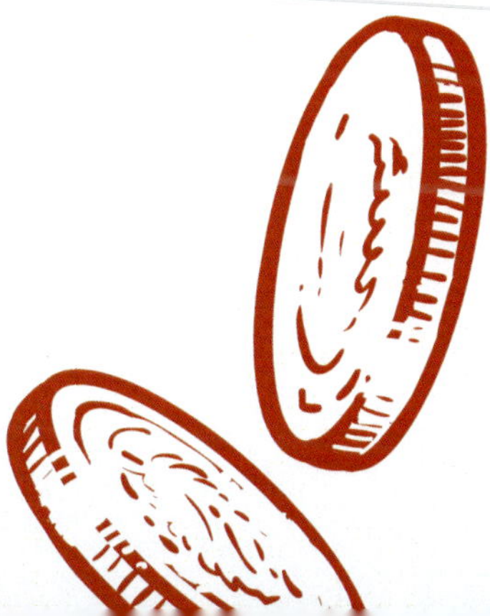

Habituators

1. Starter: Choose a regular moment when your intentional day starts. Make it a ritual. Could be the first cup of coffee, shower, commute. Create a moment where you take charge. With time you will internalise the choice process. How long does it take?

2. Here's an idea: Write a short list of catchphrases that you can believe in and use as a mantra or inner dialogue when encountering difficult people, moments or situations. (Examples: 'you got this', 'be the bigger person', 'your attitude determines your altitude' etc.)

3. Lookout: Posture is the physical manifestation of an attitude. Keep your eyes open and try to discern the attitude of others from their physical body, how they hold themselves and how they move. Use this intelligence to grow your repertoire of body language and experiment with how this changes your feelings.

4. Stretch: Let's ramp it up a bit. How can you maintain an outstanding grip on your attitude even in your most difficult moments? Plan ahead. Create a simple few steps for when you are really challenged

5. Triggers: We all have them. What are the behaviours, or situations that trigger you? Find a discerning wise friend who gets it. Ask them to challenge you to be your best self. Come up with a plan together for these triggers.

B

BIG ON BELIEF

"Successful people have fear, successful people have doubts and successful people have worries. They just don't let these stop them."

— T. Harv Eker

Belief is a mercurial quality. It can, at times be difficult to find and impossible to hold on to. Did I ever truly believe I could be Paralympic Champion? Probably not. But did I believe I could work harder than anyone else? Use the support available to me more effectively than anyone else, to give me the best chance of delivering my best performance, in that moment, to challenge for the top spot? Then yes, I certainly did.

Mohammed Ali is arguably one of the greatest sportsmen who exuded self-belief. He would enter the ring thinking: 'I'm the greatest, I'm the champion.' He never said: 'I hope I win.' This wasn't arrogance; it was backed up by his belief that he had done all the training, made all the best decisions. Meaning he was able to perform at a high standard. His positive thinking is a supplement, not a substitute, to the plan. This overt confidence may seem unattainable for some of us. And if the task we are pursuing is unknown, how can we possibly believe we are the greatest? I have learnt that the key is to believe you have the ability and that you could have done no more to be ready for that moment.

Positive thinking vs. positive believing. Positive thinking doesn't guarantee success. But coupled with positive efforts and actions, it increases our probability of success. So, if totally believing that you will succeed seems unattainable, then believe in your powers to commit to the process. Give it everything you've got and leave no stone unturned in the pursuit of that performance.

Belief is trust, faith or confidence in someone or something. This could be in yourself or in others around you, this will vary between individuals. It doesn't really matter if I don't believe in myself all the time,

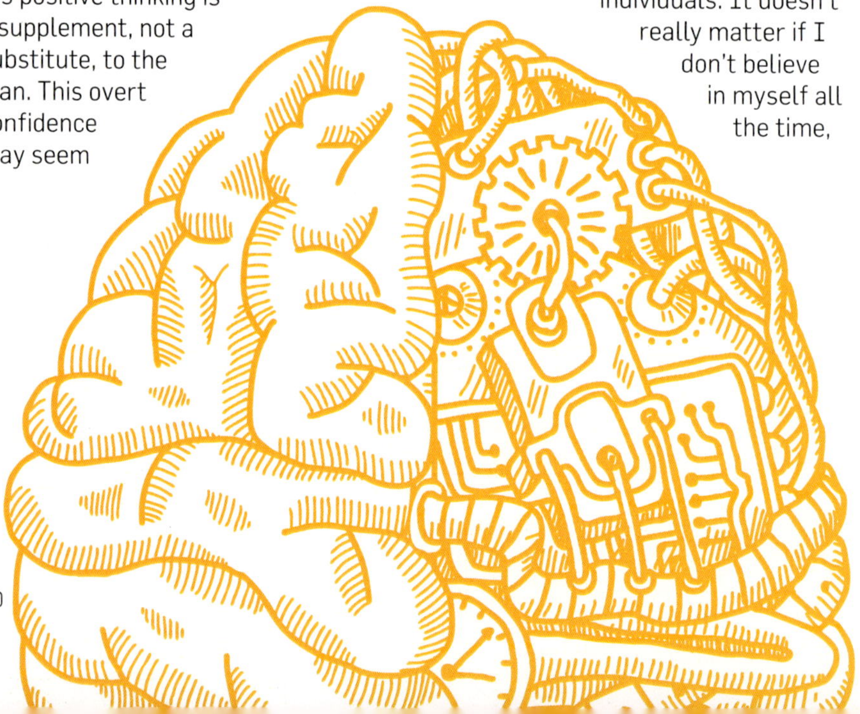

as long as I put my belief in the system, the plan and the process. This approach has worked well for me, the lack of a strong self-belief in the outcome means I leave no stone unturned in the process. During my six years unbeaten, I never lined up in the start bucket expecting to win. I took greater confidence in knowing that I had done all the training and if I focused on the process of executing my race plan, there were few in the world who would beat me. Believing we will win or be successful is very different to believing that we can do everything in our power to give us the best chance. The first is ultimately out of our control, whereas the other is 100% within our control. Also, I've always found the sometimes apparent air of confidence some folk have rather elusive. I tried for years to be more confident. To know I will win races. To be, on the day that matters, better than anyone else. To convince my coach I was oozing calm confidence. Knowing that all would be alright. Sadly, it was never something I mastered. I still wonder if it's really possible. All this taught me was that ultimately, winning is out of my control. Because the performance of others on any set day is out of my control. And actually, the most powerful factor in performing to the best of our ability is having belief that we know we have done everything we can to be ready. And believing that we are capable of delivering a performance that is good enough to challenge anyone.

One of my fundamental beliefs is that hard work, living to high standards and showing passion will result in the performances you desire. I choose to immerse myself in the belief that I can and will work hard and set high standards, rather than having to find the elusive self-belief in my own abilities. I believe that, whatever situation I find myself in, I have the abilities to cope and improve my situation through hard work and attitude.

Belief perseverance is an interesting phenomenon.

It is one where we maintain a belief despite new information that firmly contradicts it. This is a stumbling block for some and an example of where some misguided beliefs may be an inhibitor to high performance. If we have a tendency to lean towards belief perseverance we must honestly look at ourselves and try to objectively evaluate our performances on fact rather than fiction. I tend to always credit the tailwind with my good performance. And it may have played a part.

But I'm missing a valuable confidence-boosting opportunity by allowing this inaccurate assessment of my performance. We should actively seek to attribute successes, however small, to the real reasons and try to be less "British" by explaining away our good work and efforts. By doing this, we will gradually add to our self-belief stores from which we can take when things get tough.

Coaching Questions

1. Process: Believing in a certain outcome is out of your control, try believing in the process towards that outcome.

2. Doubts: Is your belief in the process, stronger than your doubts?

3. Reasons: What are the reasons you are successful?

4. Credit: Try always seeking a positive reason for success instead of the excuse. Take the credit.

5. Feel: What does your self-belief look and feel like?

Habituators

1. Examine the foundations: Work out what your belief is built on. This will help you identify what's helpful or unhelpful.

2. Identify the blockers: Is belief a blocker for you? Do you need to address it?

3. Build: What is in your control that will help build belief in the process and get you to the outcome you desire?

4. Evaluate: Evaluate any wins, however small and attribute them accurately.

5. Challenge and Change: If you don't believe in the process or plan, then question it, challenge it and change it.

CULTURE CREATION

"Culture is simply a shared way of doing something with a passion."

— Brian Chesky,
Co-Founder, CEO, Airbnb

In my work with thousands of business people I have been fascinated by the systems, and psychology at work. An emergent phenomenon, whenever humans get together, is culture. Culture doesn't exist per se. Culture arises. Culture is co-created.

Throughout our research for this book, a theme repeats time and again. Controlling the controllable. Influencing what you can. Choosing. Culture is no different. Some people are culture creators. They have the skills, know-how and mentality to shape and direct the emergent paradigm of the group. They are deliberate in how they act and speak. They are proactive in culture building, and attentive in culture nurturing. Culture is a deep instruction manual in how to operate in a specific social context.

The human social system builds from conscious and unconscious observations of the behaviour and language of others. We are master imitators and know that copying helps us fit in, gain respect, belong. Yet the words we speak, the actions we take, also impact our inner world, our thoughts, feelings and state. As individuals we are in a personal cycle. And our words and actions impact the inner world of those in our tribe.

So, there are two ways to choose culture. We can make a choice about who is in our tribe, by making smart choices about who we are connected to. Or we can create culture by choosing our words and actions, especially those that shape culture. Choosing our tribe is important. High performers across many fields hang out with those that have a positive reinforcement effect. A brilliant example is the Palo Alto poker scene. It is no surprise that the city's top entrepreneurs and top poker players, (i.e. high stakes gamblers from different fields), spend so much time together. What they have in common is a passion for understanding what constitutes a good play; how to handle the calculations and emotions of risk. What is a wise long-term and short-term strategy? Learning flows both ways. The poker players have started tech-enabled businesses and brands. The entrepreneurs (who are often great poker players) gain a sophisticated appreciation of investment strategies. We choose our tribe when we choose a job, a hobby, a church, a school, a charity partner, a team mate, a business partner. We can make choices about those individuals who will spur us on to be a better version of ourselves, in an encouraging, caring and appropriately challenging way. We can also choose to move on from people who are diminishing us where we can't get traction for change.

Choosing our words and actions is our second lever. Culture is formed of stories, language and rituals. Culture creators use these to impact themselves and others. In my organisation we have many stories, language and rituals. But I'll share just one that is a vignette about culture creation. We are very high on personal responsibility and thinking about others. So, we have a high-challenge culture. This means that in our team, you will get challenged frequently, by lots of different people. People will, if for a moment you let go, ask you to hold the standard. It can feel annoying. They are ready, with a smile, and care, to pounce. Normally with a joke to soften the blow. This plays out best in our office kitchen which is always borderline immaculate. With no real effort. Why? Everyone knows that plates should be in the dishwasher, the sink should always be empty, teabags always in the bin, full rubbish bins immediately emptied, clean dishwasher unloaded, coffee knock box emptied, milk jug

washed, steam wand properly cleaned. I'm very proud of how the conversations go. First a photo of the offense on Slack. And then one message: 'Own up. Who did this?' Tough love. There is a dedicated ongoing story, with illustrations, of how similar and close the bin is to the sink, and a story of bafflement that people could be so lazy they couldn't step the one metre it takes to put the teabag in the bin. So, the teabag is the story. The challenge is the ritual. The directness and humour is the language. And this whole narrative is an icon. A pattern. We have the toolkit to challenge each other to hold the highest standard in every area of our work. The teabag narrative works for every other area, performance, timekeeping, honesty, career, stretch. Teabags and kitchens are a practice ground for everything else that matters. So, find your teabags.

As we go from the kitchen into more important aspects of our work, we find the same phenomena at play. Culture is (almost) everything. We have worked with hundreds of teams. The successful teams have a clear culture. Period. The cultures are not always the same. One type of culture does not work for every organisation. But the culture gives each team a unique identity.

We have spent a great deal of time working with the BMW Group over 20 years. The strapline 'The ultimate driving machine' contains both what they do; driving machines, but also 'ultimate'; things have to be excellent. From the shine of the floor, to the wheel nuts on the car. This is the kind of company where everything has to be outstanding. The cultural value bonds the people into a belief system. And the belief system creates a sense of togetherness. A tribe.

Coaching Questions

1. People: Who are the culture creators around you?

2. Culture: What is the culture that will best support your success?

3. Changes: If you could change one aspect of the culture you are in, what would you change?

4. Excellence: What does a culture of excellence mean for you or your organisation?

5. Shape: How can you become a person who shapes culture?

Habituators

1. Patterns: Have a play with the cultural patterns that exist around you. Changing one dimension may have unexpected positive impacts elsewhere. Explore the connections.

2. Words: Identify the key words of your culture. Write them down. It could be stories, phrases, or expressions.

3. Reinforcement: Choose an element of culture to positively reinforce and amplify.

4. Reset: Take some time to work out what team culture you would create if you were starting from scratch. Identify from first principles: What is important for the success of your tribe?

5. Escape: Go visit other cultures. Teams, countries, organisations. Immerse yourself in some alternative cultures.

Having a strong organisational company culture can positively permeate into our everyday lives. A synthesis by the US National Institute of Health of 62 studies "found a consistently positive association" in 74.2% of studies between healthcare facilities whose activities promote a positive culture and patient outcomes, such as reduced mortality rates, increased patient satisfaction and a decrease in depression rates.

* Undertaken to provide information for healthcare policy makers, the synthesis defined positive culture as one which was cohesive, supportive, collaborative and inclusive in nature.* 'Association between organisational and workplace cultures, and patient outcomes: systematic review', National Institute of Health's National Library of Medicine (Nov, 2017)

DRIVES AND DESIRE

"Effort and courage are not enough without purpose and direction."

— John F Kennedy

Drive can be defined as an urge or a force to move in a specified direction. This can vary in people. Some are more driven than others. Some have strong internal drivers, for example, pursuit of knowledge, mastery or enjoyment. Others are driven by external factors such as money, rewards or recognition by others. It is often down to the individual themselves as to which drivers are more powerful. There is no set recipe for which source of drive is better for success. But in my opinion, it is likely that internal drivers are more resistant to the challenges we may face in the pursuit of high performance. However, one thing that we can all agree on is that drive is essential for high performance.

So, if we all agree that drive is important and that people have it in different amounts, where's the win? Where can we make a change to have a performance impact for ourselves? I believe it is in the direction of the drive. It would be easy to appear driven in all that we do. Staying up late. Being first in the office. Volunteering for tasks. Piling more and more on our plates. But does this equate to successful performance? Probably not. In fact the key is in understanding how we can direct our drive to maximise our performances. This may differ with the various performance moments we experience. But fundamentally, we can ask ourselves some simple questions to help us direct our drive and our next actions;

Where do I want to end up?

Will this activity or task positively add to my end goal?

Do I have the time / energy to do this?

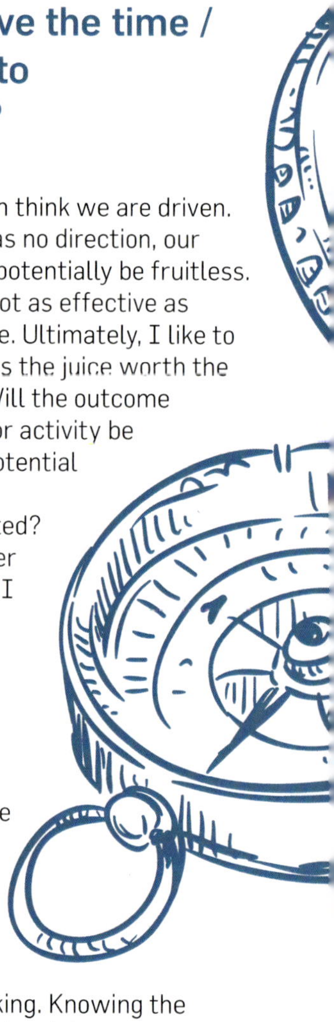

We can often think we are driven. But if this has no direction, our efforts will potentially be fruitless. Or at best, not as effective as they could be. Ultimately, I like to ask myself 'is the juice worth the squeeze?'. Will the outcome of any task or activity be worth the potential effort and energy exerted? If the answer is 'yes', then I have a clear direction in which to focus my drive – and off I go. Equally, if the answer is 'no', it gives us some real clarity to our decision making. Knowing the plan, the goal and the process are vital to success and will help apply our 'drive' in a more purposeful way. A real game changer was when I directed my drive to all areas of my performance. It can be easy to be driven in the obvious moments; the gym, the lake or indeed, the office. But it was only when I became equally focused on my rest and recovery, that I saw a leap; not only in the gains I made, but in the energy I had available for other important moments. So, don't neglect the less obvious areas of your performance; nutrition, hydration, rest and recovery. By applying the same questioning to these you just might see further performance gains.

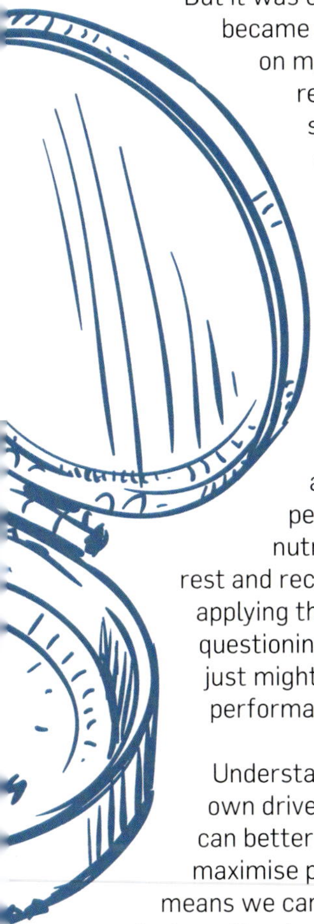

Understanding our own drive and how we can better direct it to maximise performance means we can potentially unlock another key aspect of performance; desire. If our desire to complete something is high we can then utilise our drive to complete it to a higher standard. As a consequence we will see better results plus we enjoy the journey more along the way.

What if the desire is not there? Imagine the tasks that we all have to do but don't always enjoy. The necessary but dull bits and bobs of life that can, and will, positively impact performance if we get them right. The challenge here is; how do you find desire if the task at hand, and direction required, doesn't float your boat? ('scuse the pun). In this instance, I believe understanding the purpose and potential value of the task allows us to build the required desire and drive to complete it to a high standard. It's all about self-care, really. Taking some time to do the less exciting tasks that will look after us and allow us the extra energy to complete the tasks we really desire. We will reap the rewards of feeling empowered. More energetic. Happier. Not to mention a little bit smug when we don't have to reach for that pre-packed meal or sugary snack, which would only smack us in the face with a sugar low just when we need to focus.

In essence, drive and desire are fundamental to each other and to high performance. By unlocking our ability to both understand and influence the direction of each, we ultimately seek out challenges in which to test or prove our abilities, be more content with our efforts and endeavours and give ourselves a greater chance of succeeding in our moment.

Coaching Questions

1. Focus: What can you focus your drive on (and control) that will impact your performance?

2. Juice: Is the juice worth the squeeze?

3. Control: Under how much of your control are the outcomes you seek?

4. Desire: Are your desires easily fuelled by your drivers?

5. Drive: Have you got a clear focus to direct your drive?

Habituators

1. List: Make a list of your drivers and put the list in priority order.

2. Consequence: What are the consequences of not achieving success? Does the task really matter?

3. Share: Understand what drives you and share this with your team or colleagues. For example, passion for success may lead to a questioning approach that others may find annoying, without knowing that the driver is a passion to be competent and understand.

4. Propagate: Are you applying your drive to all aspects of your performance? E.g. how driven are you to ensure you are well fed, hydrated and recovered with quality sleep?

5. Plan: Work out a clear plan or process to 'Focus your drive and then drive your focus.'

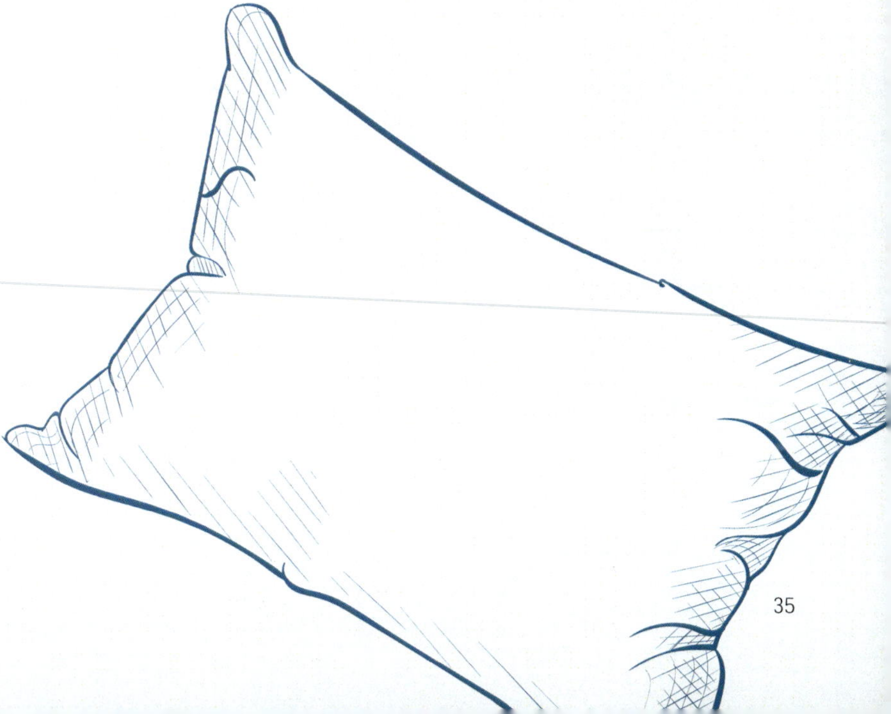

ELEVATING ENDURANCE

"Do not pray for an easy life, pray for the strength to endure a difficult one."

— Bruce Lee

Popular definitions may suggest that "resilience" is the ability to 'get by' in psychologically challenging circumstances whereas "endurance" infers a more physical aspect, with a more rigid mindset where we're continually pushing our body (and mind) through hardship without giving up. Arguably, I would say that they are both sides of the same coin.

But, as with resilience (see Chapter 18, *Responsibility, Resilience and the Rough Stuff*), I believe that endurance is often about maintaining flexible thinking, balancing available personal resources, and being adaptable to what's happening around us. Being able to identify and manage available personal resources effectively will almost certainly define how well we endure and whether we will just survive or thrive. Below is a list of some basic resources. Some of them are perhaps stating the obvious but are certainly worth further consideration if we wish to elevate our levels of endurance.

Human Resources – what we need:

1. Air

Clearly, without air we die but the art of breathing effectively is something that we, as humans, aren't always very good at. Learning to breathe well can help us overcome many obstacles, such as increased stress levels and poor sleep. For instance, if feeling stressed or angry, breathing out stimulates the relaxation response and helps us calm down.

2. Food and Water

It may sound obvious, but staying hydrated and maintaining a balanced diet will aid endurance. Foods containing tryptophan, such as milk, oats and certain nuts are good for sleep. Hydrating with a glass of water when you wake up helps rehydrate the body and brain (see Chapter 19, *Slips, Setbacks and Sucking it Up*) and aids physical and psychological recovery.

3. Shelter

In extreme conditions, having some form of physical shelter is really important. Finding somewhere or something to 'protect' us from the elements is vital for enduring (a home, a car, a coat or a tarpaulin under a tree).

4. Attitude

A positive and proactive attitude is key to human endurance (see Chapter 1, *Attitude at Altitude*). Beware of blind optimism: 'It'll be alright in the end' or 'It's meant to be' don't always work out the way you hoped they would!

5. Social Connection

Humans need other people. Having people we can trust and feel safe with helps us all get through tough times. Social connection (i.e. touch, sex, social identity etc) is widely considered to be the No.1 factor in human resilience and is covered throughout this book. Those that can get along, will almost certainly endure longer.

6. Safety (Psychological and / or Physical)

As well as having physical shelter, we also need somewhere that offers us psychological safety. This can be with another trusted person, or group, or a place where you can be true and honest to yourself without threat of retribution. Finding a safe place is essential for sustained endurance and can be through practising mindfulness on the side of a mountain or sitting in the car on the way to or from work.

7. Purpose

Having a meaningful purpose is central to effective endurance (see Chapter 9, *Ikigai*).

8. General Health and Wellbeing

Maintenance of health and wellbeing is key to living a full life. Obviously, we can't always predict the future and we are all susceptible to illness and ailments. But if we invest time and effort into looking after ourselves physically, mentally and emotionally through exercise, correct posture, regular breaks, active recovery; talking to trusted others, decompression, etc, we give ourselves the best chance of effective endurance.

This list is not exhaustive but it should give you a good starting point.

If your resources are sufficient and accessible and your positive attitude engaged and flexible, then there is a good chance that you will be able to successfully endure most things, recover after the ordeal and hopefully learn something along the way too. Learning to push ourselves is something most of us experience from an early age so there is already an expectation that you are likely to face challenges in life. At the very least, we all know that we will have to, dig in, from time to time when things get tough. Life is hopefully a long game and our ability to persevere through suffering is what takes us to new places.

So, to give yourself the best chance of effective endurance, wherever and whenever it's needed, anticipate it (if you can) and prepare for it. Some people, me included, find it really useful to break this process down into phases:

Before (Preparation)

What do we need to do to best prepare ourselves for what we're about to undertake or face? This can be a short-term or long-term goal, but it means that we are consciously giving 'it' some thought, which in turn, builds our confidence.

During (Performance)

How do I maintain personal awareness of myself and others (team, family etc.) and manage available resources effectively? What are my dynamic coping strategies; short term and long term for managing self-regulation of increased stress levels, or anxiety etc.? When do I actively engage with putting effort in and when do I rest (foot on the accelerator/foot on the brake). Where is my safe place, just in case?

After (Recovery)

What lessons have I learned? What do I now need to do to recover and get ready for the next challenge? Rest and recuperation are really important for elevated endurance but can be done effectively along the way and in small chunks rather than longer periods of relaxation after the event. This is active recovery and can include strategies such as napping in the day (see Chapter 26, *Zzzs*) or taking a two-minute breather (diaphramatic breathing) in the fresh air.

Luckily, most people do have the capacity to endure far more than they think. After all, humans are generally resilient. It's just that some of our resources are kept in reserve. We often only get access to them subconsciously when we most need them. But the resources are there. Learning to know how far we can push ourselves and learning how to self-regulate and manage resources is vital for functional endurance. It can be liberating to know what being at our limit feels like mentally, emotionally and physically. It also allows us to work out, through personally developed strategies, how we consciously access the reserves we have in order to effectively self-regulate and endure.

The military can provide a really good example of readying people for endurance. Teams responsible for training recruits know that the tests they're going to face are sometimes going to be very tough. So they ensure that recruits learn what personal and practical resources are required for potential tasks

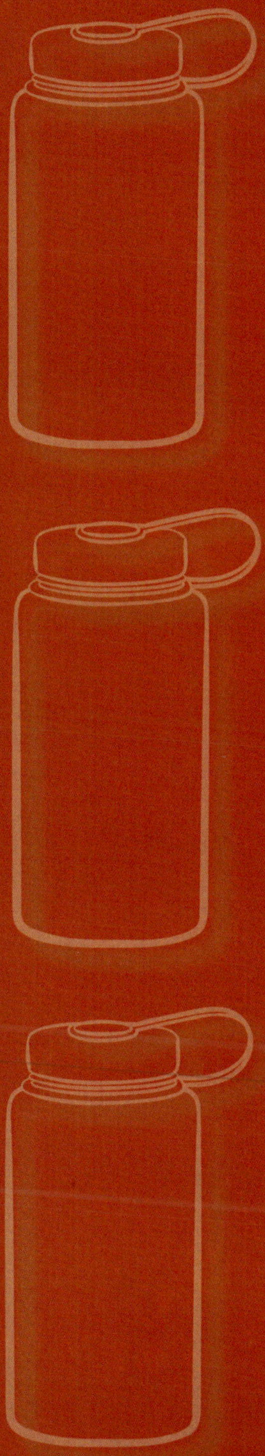

to be faced. They front-load essential resources such as sufficient water and food (including extra emergency rations), spare clothing and a shelter for sleeping under. Material basics for getting by when things are tough. Even if recruits don't actually end up using them, their personal endurance-potential has been increased simply because they feel prepared and thus more confident in their ability to perform under pressure. Ready for the challenge. Again, it's a choice. But it's taught during training so that active service personnel are better mission-prepared to endure, both physically and mentally. Clearly the practice described here is not only limited to military service and the tenets can be applied to many other scenarios.

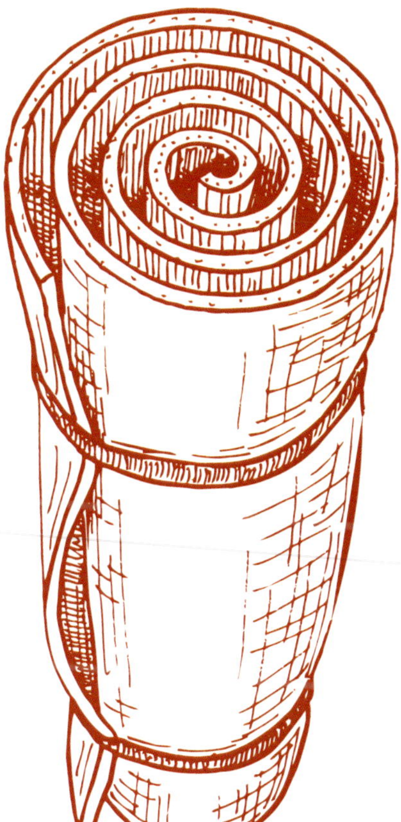

A number of years ago I ran The Marathon des Sables, reportedly the toughest footrace on Earth. I am no great runner, but it was on my bucket list, so when I was invited by a friend, I readily accepted. On the fourth day of the race, and halfway up a rather large sand dune, I recall a conversation between my friend and a young Canadian (I was too tired to talk at the time). The Canadian was an accomplished ultra-runner but he was clearly struggling in the intensely hot and sandy conditions.

As we plodded on upwards, he kept looking at his huge watch, which I took for a GPS (amongst other things). As we navigated the dunes, I noted that, each time he looked at the watch, he seemed more and more anxious. The watch was actually a heart rate monitor, which was perhaps subconsciously telling him that if he didn't stop immediately, his heart would likely explode and he would die! We tried to reassure him that he needed to listen to his body rather than focus on his watch (which was clearly increasing his stress levels). As we continued, we explained that remaining aware of why we were there and what was happening within ourselves, would enable us to maintain personal, flexible strategies for copying. These would allow us to walk when we felt tired of running, run when we felt good or rest (even for a short period) if we were feeling overwhelmed or knackered. This ability to remain adaptable and have the confidence to trust our bodies (even to stop) and take one small step at a time when needed, meant that we could endure happier for longer. When we worry, our body releases cortisol. In turn, this can affect confidence and ultimately undo performance, sliding into a negative belief cycle. When you don't feel in control, this can be a difficult cycle to break. Sadly, the young ultra-runner withdrew the next day, blaming his poor blistered feet.

Coaching Questions

1. Strategise: What personal strategies do you have in place in order to face the days challenges (i.e. to deal with challenging conversations or elevated stress levels?

2. Move: Do you have the ability to be physically active during the day? If not, how can you fit this in? If so, how?

3. Strength: What do you think is your greatest strength?

4. Weakness: What do you think is your biggest weakness?

5. Advise: If you could give one piece of advice on how best to maintain personal/team endurance, what would it be?

Habituators

1. Goals: Prepare for short term/long term goals.

2. Breathe: Have strategies that help you manage increased stress levels or overwhelm. Breathing strategies such as two minutes of deep, diaphragmatic breathing can help.

3. Quick: Practise short-term activities to relieve stress, such as box breathing when stopped at traffic lights in your car or before delivering an important talk or piece of news. Box breathing: (breathe out through your mouth for four seconds – hold your breath for four seconds – breathe in through your nose for four seconds – hold your breath for four seconds. Repeat for two minutes, or as long as it takes for you to notice the change.

4. Snack-pack: If out for a walk or in the car, carry healthy snacks and water.

5. Hydrate: The first drink of the morning should be a glass of water to rehydrate the brain.

A study in Science Advances by Duke University examined the limits of human endurance. Analysing elite athletic events and extreme activity, findings indicated that **the body cannot digest, absorb and process enough calories and nutrients to sustain a higher level of sustainable energy use than 2.5 times the resting metabolic rate.** During pregnancy, women's energy peaks at 2.2 times.

*'Extreme events reveal an alimentary limit on sustained maximal human energy expenditure

FLEXIBILITY, FREEDOM AND FUN

"Freedom is the open window through which pours the sunlight of the human spirit and human dignity."

— Herbert Hoover

Adaptability and flexibility in behaviour, as well as mindset, are part of what it is to be human. In a fast-paced, ever-changing world, having the ability to maintain awareness of self, others and the changing environment is essential.

Most importantly, having the belief that we have the necessary skills, knowledge and suitable attitude or mindset to deal with what faces us brings the confidence required to face future challenges, and not see them as threats.

In life, so many, many things will happen that are unexpected. With a sense of flexibility and freedom we are able to adapt. In my business life, I choose the metaphor of surfing as an analogy. The waves will keep coming. New clients. New projects. New team members. New products. New processes. And setbacks. People issues. Strategy problems. Cashflow issues. Client problems. The question is whether we can notice what's happening, and adapt. Can we quickly orientate our mind and body, adapt our posture (whether literally or metaphorically)? Very often we will spend months preparing a leadership training only for the client to get an 'exciting last-minute idea'. To perform at our highest level, we must be ready to joyfully embrace this idea and ride it all the way to the brought course, whilst riding, we can still steer. We have some input to the process. When we are really in the groove with flexibility and freedom we give away part of our need to control life, other people and events. It's a truly empowering experience, akin to travelling with a friend, but letting them set the agenda at any given moment. During the 2020 Covid-19 crisis our business was hit pretty hard. Some of our advisors suggested working flat out, and extremely hard, to try to maintain revenues. I saw it differently. Why fight the wave when we can go with it? Why not take a hit on revenue, why push water up hill in sales? When life deals you lemons, (joyfully, I say) make lemonade. We abandoned the goals set during the good times and got some other goals in place. Don't go bankrupt. Don't lose money. But why not take it easy for a few months after so many years of flat-out work? Why not surf the wave?

Less work. Less Money. Less Security. More fun. More cycling. More family. More suntan. Unfettered by the railroads of corporate goals, why not treat this as a pivot point, an innovation moment, and surf this huge tsunami to.... a completely different beach. I watched many corporate people grind out horrendous 12-hour days, trying to live their old life. And our team did work hard. But with a mission to keep the company running so we could enjoy the good times when they returned. And in the meantime, explore this new playground while being on a new journey to who-knows-where.

Part of what limits our freedom and flexibility is ego. Ego can make us push for what we said we would do. I had a friend who, age 21, was in a successful band. By age 31, with kids on the way, he was ready to leave. He wanted a new life. But was trapped with his previous commitment to himself and others: 'We will never quit'. It took some careful unpicking to get clear that the ego of a 21-year-old, who wants to make it, can't drive the decisions of a 31-year-old with a kid on the way. Ego is a funny thing. It tells us what we must or must not do. For appearances. I know executives who have quashed their freedom and dreams and stayed in limiting jobs because they wanted to have the right company car on the drive to impress their neighbours. Choose life. Even if it's not what you planned.

Do we have the skills to go with what is happening? Are we able to ride the wave, adapt, flex, switch, pivot? After all, is life not an adventure? Are adventures not comprised of escapades? Are escapades not, after all, moments where not all went well; we had a near-miss, a close-call, or an actual-bad-thing happened? Maintaining a playfulness in escapades, setback, the adventure of life, is what allows us to laugh at our situation, even if it's bleak or difficult. And that playfulness is a safety net that means we can push ourselves to our absolute limits. We can take risks. Be bold. Courageous. Knowing that if the worst happens, well, life is an experience.

Coaching Questions

1. Flex: What is flexing in your life right now? How?

2. Build: How can you build a muscle that allows you to go with and accept change?

3. Network: Who in your circle demonstrates adaptability? What can you learn from them?

4. Adapt: How is your adaptability impacted when you are under pressure? What can you do to build flexibility even under pressure?

5. Play: What brings you fun and how can you create more of that?

Habituators

1. Super basic: Wear your watch on the other wrist for a week. So weird.

2. Who me? Change how you introduce yourself to new people. See how it impacts them, and you.

3. Break the rules: Not the law or moral code. Go to the cinema in the working day. That kind of thing. Stay up too late. What do you notice?

4. Say 'yes': When you would normally say 'no'. A strategy from the book Yes Man by Danny Wallace. So fun.

5. Focus on capabilities: When a challenge occurs, list the skills you have to meet the challenge.

A study of 107 companies and 15,164 participating employees by the University of Konstanz highlighted that **'it is not employees' chronological age but their subjective age**, a factor that can be influenced, **which drives organisational performance outcomes'.**

*'It Matters How Old You Feel – Antecedents and Performance Consequences of Average Relative Subjective-Age in Organisations', Journal of Applied Psychology (2015)

GOALS AND GROWTH

"If you focus on goals, you may achieve goals, but that doesn't guarantee growth.

If you focus on growth, you will grow and always hit goals."

— John C. Maxwell

Human beings are generally resilient. We are because, as a species, we have developed the ability to learn from past events. Whether it's learning from catastrophic mistakes or surprising successes, we have the ability to apply the knowledge and wisdom gained in preparation for what may lay ahead. Having set aims, objectives and an optimistic outlook is generally good for us all. But when we are able to focus on particular desired outcomes and formulate pragmatic approaches to reach those outcomes, we as humans most often have the ability to achieve great things. These desired outcomes are also termed as goals and can be used to describe something that is quickly achievable, something that may take time to accomplish and something way-off in the future or something in between.

Goal:

The object of a person's ambition or effort; an aim or desired result or a desire or drive to move from where you are now to somewhere better.

Humans not only dream of past experiences but we have the ability to creatively plan for the future, something most animals are incapable of. This often starts with a thought, a feeling or an "itch", but with some consideration and imagination, these can be moulded into a positive idea, desire and importantly, a plan, where we can put the idea into action and actually do something. Coaching, which is a future-focused intervention (i.e. not dwelling on past happenings), is centred around the idea of reaching goals. A way of looking at self-coaching is to say: 'This is where I am now' (current situation). 'That's where I want to go to' (outcome or goal). And: 'This is how I'm going to get there.' Including choices available (and potential consequences) and a plan of what to do (actions).

Knowing that, in life, we have a need and a desire to learn from experiences, the drive to achieve personal or collective goals and grow along the way is, at a basic level, key to human survival. To progress or lead a meaningful life. Add a positive and flexible, yet robust, attitude to the mix and we're looking more likely to achieve our determined goals. As humans, we learn when things are good and we feel safe. When we feel psychologically safe (where our values and beliefs aren't compromised) we know that we can learn and grow when things don't necessarily go our way, too. Even learning to grow following adversity and trauma is possible. This is known as having a growth mindset and it's a really useful asset when facing a world of change and uncertainty and still wanting to perform under pressure and achieve meaningful goals.

In coaching we often use the analogy of a young child seeing fire for the first time, who, in exploring its draw and beauty, gets burnt. If the child decides that fire is too dangerous to even go near again, then growing up with no warmth, cooked food and comfort would be tough, to say the least.

On the other hand, if the child realises that they only get burnt if they get too close, then they can take active measures to protect themself whilst enjoying the huge benefits and beauty of fire. In this case, the child has practised experiential learning in order to grow as a person. How many Neanderthals, on first meeting fire or lava, had a similar experience and perhaps missed the opportunity to live a happier life?

As stated, humans grow most and learn more effectively when they feel psychologically safe. When in a state of perceived safety, our bodies are flooded with positive hormones like dopamine, serotonin, endorphins and oxytocin which enable and encourage us to enjoy the moment and appreciate the people around us, test new personal theories and push ourselves, even to the limits. When we feel unsafe, a feeling, driven by our senses, combined with the memory of previous experiences, causes our body to be flooded with the stress-related hormone cortisol. This is laced with adrenaline to ensure it gets to all the right places as quickly as possible, often before we are even consciously aware, with the sole purpose of getting you to do something, which is often referred to as the Flight, Fight or Freeze response. In this state we may feel anxious, nervous or scared and may become rather risk averse, preventing us from trying out those new things or pushing ourselves, even to escape harm. This is a place where many of us get stuck.

For some, this becomes an unpleasant place to be, often leaving us feeling depressed or worried and without the personal resources we sometimes find ourselves unable to climb out of the ditch we've found ourselves in.

During mobilisation, or fight or flight phase, the bodily aim is to recover to a place of perceived safety. While feeling unsafe, we can enter a stressed state, when our body concentrates on little but survival or, at best, getting through tough times. In order to learn effectively and grow as a person we need to feel that we are safe. This does not necessarily mean physically safe. Over the years, I have found myself in some really testing environments. In truth, I rarely felt frightened or scared. Nervous, perhaps but rarely more than anxious. I don't put this down to me being extraordinarily brave. It was more the fact that I was doing something that I believed in and that I was most often surrounded by capable friends and colleagues that have a similar attitude to me.

In those moments, I may have been far from being physically safe but I was psychologically safe. And for me, that was okay. Looking back, it seems rather absurd. Even though the greatest drive for a human being is one of

Forms of Adversarial or Post Traumatic Growth

survival, we can put one's beliefs and sense of purpose ahead of personal physical safety. I figure that the drive for meaningful existence and survival of the human species can be entwined with the needs of a single person and encourage us to forge ahead, achieve those goals and learn and grow along the way, even in the most challenging of environments.

Coaching Questions

1. Success: Consider a time you achieved your goals. What did you learn from that experience?

2. Emotion: How did the experience make you feel?

3. Safety: How safe did you feel during the experience (physically or/and psychologically)?

4. Context: Where, or with whom, do you feel safe?

5. Next: What is your next goal to focus on?

Habituators

1. Score: Give yourself a score (from 1-10) on how you generally feel at that moment and come up with one thing that you can do today that will increase that score by at 1.

2. Chunk: Break down big goals into small, bite-size chunks, to not feel overwhelmed.

3. Improve: Consider areas of your life that you would like to work on or improve.

4. Rhythm: Try to find one activity that helps ground you during a period of flux or uncontrollability (deep rhythmic breathing, exercise, count to 10).

5. Explore: Learn the factors of Post Traumatic Growth. There is lots of other great writing and research out there.

The American Academy of Neurology conducted a series of tests which revealed that **those with the highest levels of the stress-related hormone cortisol performed worse on tests of memory, organisation, visual perception and attention.** Performed on 2,231 participants (sample was 53.2% female), the cognitive tests primarily measured the volume of white and grey matter to determine their results.*

* Eschouffo-Tcheugui, Justin B. et al, 'Circulating cortisol and cognitive and structural brain measures The Framingham Heart Study' (2018)

HOLISTIC THINKING

"You gotta nourish in order to flourish."

— Author Unknown

Early in my career, I trained under a psychotherapist called Ian. Ian introduced me to the life wheel that I've used with hundreds of senior execs since.

Life Balance

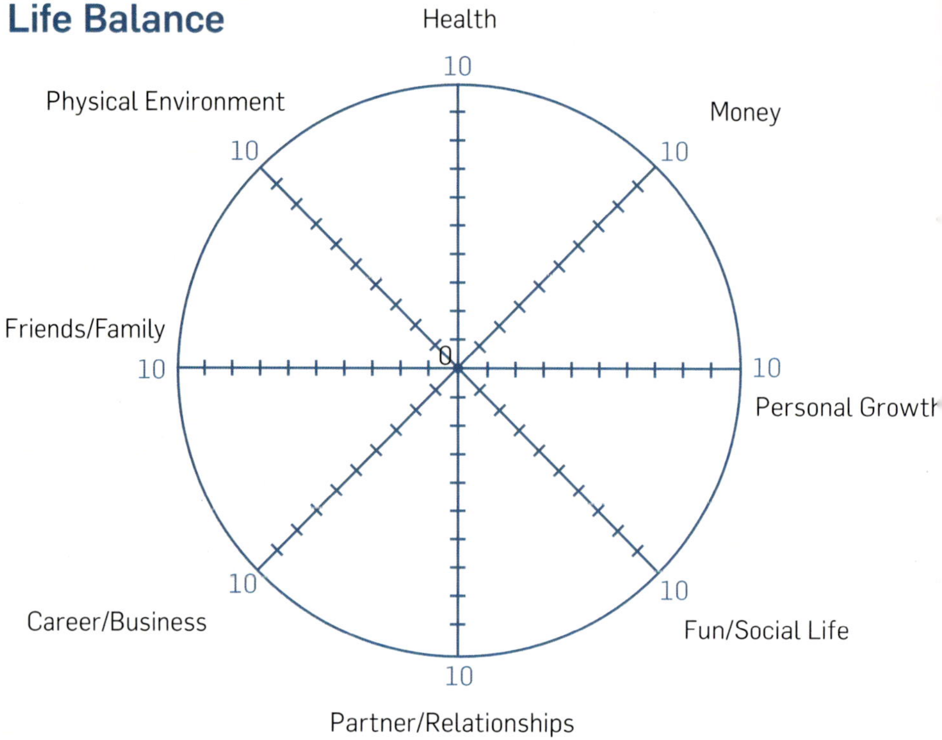

Under Ian's guidance we worked as individuals to define:

Where am I (scored from 10) and What do I want more of in this area?

Then we had to work out how to reach our goals, without negatively impacting other areas of our life. The life balance wheel is just one tool. But at the time it had a big impact on me. I had been pursuing success at work. Personal growth. Success with money. But had been missing out on fun, friends, health, and was single. In essence, I was making trade-offs. We all do, from time to time. And in the short term, trade-offs can help us succeed by providing focus. Yet a creeping sense of dissatisfaction can come in when these trade-offs start to stack up for too long, or in too many areas.

Considering the holistic nature of the performance we are seeking is vital to our success. There are many factors that impact upon performance and it's only when we consider all of these and establish how much attention to pay them that we will have the opportunity to really reach those performance heights. Considering ourselves as a whole rather than a single facet is vital. That includes the social dimension of life. We are a part of our community, our family, our marriage or partnership, our business partnership.

Looking after all aspects of our life and determining what takes precedent will ultimately help us perform better. Making sure that our family or friends are aligned with our life choices and can be cheerleaders and supporters rather than critics. And equally, making sure our own life choices are aligned with theirs too, so that everything in the system works. Holistic thinking is also to bring all our resources to bear when considering aspects of our life. To harness physical, emotional, mental, spiritual inner resources and thinking style.

When I was working in Saudi Arabia, I met one man who shared his problem-solving approach. 'I go to the mosque for a sleep' he said. 'When I wake, the solution is normally clear.' Holistic thinking, using all of our senses, bringing all of our personal toolbox to bear. My friend was using his subconscious, and cues from his faith, and resting his body to unleash his best problem solving. Using everything at our disposal. Using absolutely everything we've got. To make life as effective as possible, we are relying on everything that we are, and can do, to bring ourselves into the best life possible. An example is in decision making; whether to make a gut decision or a head decision. Head decisions can be a bit behind gut decisions. Trusting our instincts is a method of information gathering.

Synthesis

We often see people prepared to accept far too difficult trade-offs that ultimately undermine high performance. Overtraining or overworking are classic examples. Enduring an extremely long commute, to dutifully trudge to a highly-paid job, to pay a mortgage or school fees but never see the very kids you are aiming to raise, is a another. The antidote is working out how to synthesise. Can you combine a business trip with visits to friends and family? Can you commute by bike or jogging, even part of the way?

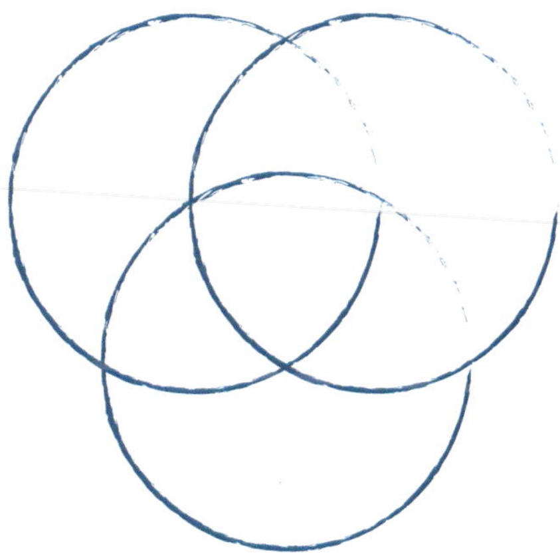

Can you work with friends? Can you explore your personal growth through your career? Can you take a holiday that keeps you active? Can work be fun? Can your partner share your passions? Or the reverse: Can you and your partner have very separate hobbies so that in pursuing them you get me-time or a different social mix. I used to feel guilty about my extensive business travel. Until my wife said one day: 'I love it when you are away. I get to go to bed late, watch crap TV, have a quiet house to myself and in the morning, everything is where I left it. You get to have an adventure, see a new part of the world, hang out with different people and come back refreshed.' I had an epiphany, about the holistic benefits of time away on the whole system of our lives. Going away was a big-picture benefit, even if it was a small-picture trade-off.

Coaching Questions

1. Wholesome: How can you adapt life to make it work better as a whole?

2. Trade-offs: Where do you feel you are currently making trade-offs and how can you turn this into synthesis or symbiosis?

3. Balance: What are the concrete actions you can take to improve each area of the balance wheel?

4. Simplify: What can you do to simplify your life?

5. Connect: Who else is important to you and how can you help them get their life in balance?

Habituators

1. Reconnect: Make one call per week to someone you haven't properly kept in touch with.

2. Exercise: Identify a fulfilling next step in your exercise life and commit to it.

3. Money: Do a financial review and see where your finances are leaking. Take action to plug the holes.

4. Career: Invest time in developing a new skill. New capabilities lead to new places and new choices. Pick something. Work on it.

5. Max Fun: Build in a bit more fun in life. Frivolity. Hilarity. Something that will leave you and those around you with big smiles on their faces.

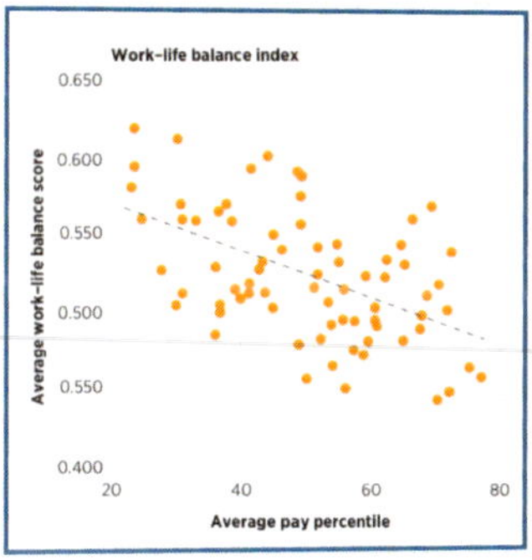

The 2020 UK Working Lives survey, conducted in January 2020 by CIPD, the professional body for HR and people development, found that **higher-paying occupations have a negative correlation with self-perceived work-life balance.** This was a finding from of 6,681 workers representative of the UK as a whole grading their working life against seven indices.*

*Quotas were used to target the sample and subsequent weights based on ONS figures were applied to the dataset. The sample is representative of the UK workforce in terms of gender, full- or part-time work status, organisation size within each sector, and industry. Work-life balance areas included overwork, commuting time, how much work encroaches on personal life and vice versa, and HR provision for flexible working.

IKIGAI

"Unless a kernel of wheat falls to the ground and dies, it remains only a single seed. But if it dies, it produces many seeds."

– John 12:24

Having purpose in life is considered vitally important in living a fulfilling life. It doesn't necessarily need to be happy, healthy or prosperous in terms of what you see, but it needs to be something that makes you feel that you're doing something bigger than you . Most people that want to get on in life have, at some point, a meaningful sense of purpose. I also believe, through a number of years coaching, that not everyone is willing to commit to a sense of purpose that truly motivates and drives us. Finding a purpose, whether stumbling upon it by accident or by good or bad fortune, requires responsibility, ownership and nurturing to bring to fruition. For some of us, that purpose needs to be in words; written down, a manifesto, a vision. For others, finding our purpose is simply a feeling, an inner conviction that we are on the right track.

Ikigai is a Japanese concept meaning 'reason for being'. It's an interesting idea. Perhaps a question. Can you find what you love, that the world needs, that you are good at and that you can get paid for? When one of those strands is missing, we experience some inner loss. Let's imagine we have a job we are good at, that the world needs, and we get paid for, but that we don't love. We may then feel comfortable, but have feelings of emptiness. We meet many people in this situation in their careers. Finding a purpose, a North Star, an inner compass, can help us navigate the tricky times in our life.

For a phase of my life my friends called me the dream killer. The irony was, I had spent years training as a business coach and had even been challenged by a mentor to 'stop encouraging people so much because it seems disingenuous'.

How could a super-positive, optimistic and trained coach be a dream killer? Partly the answer is in ikigai. At the time I had many friends who followed the orthodoxy that: 'If you work hard enough at your passion you will make it.' 'Never give up and you will achieve your dreams.' 'Don't sell out to the man.' Our culture is full of what I now know to be survivor bias.

Survivorship bias or survival bias is the logical error of concentrating on the people or things that made it past some selection process and overlooking those that did not; typically because of their lack of viability. This can lead to false conclusions in several different ways. It is a form of selection bias. So, when Kim and Kanye say: 'Hey, if you don't give up on your dreams you can make it like us' we can't believe them. There's only one Kim, only one Kanye. There's only one world champion every year. Only one gold medalist every four. Only one Elon Musk. Only one Jeff Bezos. So, the dream killer would say to his friends: 'You probably aren't going to make it in music, acting, entrepreneurship, etc. It's very likely that you will pursue what you love, but does the world need it? Are you going to get paid for it?' (Even I was tactful enough to avoid the question 'Are you really any good at it?') Dream killing was my way of saying: 'I don't want you to feel useless, have no wealth, have emptiness, or a continual sense of uncertainty.' It was also my way of saying: 'There may only be one Kanye, but there's also only one of you.' What do you want with your life? What are you good at? Not dreams, but what the world needs. What you can get paid for?

One of the greatest people I had this chat with over the years was my business partner, Andy. An amazing musician. Hard working. Dedicated. He toured. Played massive gigs in Hyde Park. Was on Radio 2. Made albums. But at the same time the work was unstable. The money unreliable. I'm not sure Andy found his purpose in the classic epiphany. But he did find what he was good at. He is a performer. He does love travelling the world running workshops packed full of interesting execs. The world does need his wisdom on leadership, storytelling, how to be a better person. And you can get paid for it. Neither Andy nor I am overly into these find-your-purpose people. Yet we have both found ours. It's better than dreams. Because it's real. As the parable says, sometimes we have to let the seed fall to the ground and die. And out of that, our real purpose can appear, and go on to create many seeds.

Coaching Questions

1. Purpose: What do you see as your purpose(s) in life at this moment?

2. Talent: What things are you really good at?

3. Passion: What things do you love to do?

4. Cash: How much money do you need to make in a year to be satisfied?

5. Contribution: What can you contribute to the world in general, or your local community?

Habituators

1. Life review: In what seasons were you really fulfilled in the past?

2. Find a friend: Who would be a good mentor in a journey towards a more meaningful life?

3. Experiment: What can you try that will increase your life fulfilment in the next month? Give some time to something you value.

4. Get Good: 'What you are good at?' is pretty vague. Identify the skill sets that you would like to truly master. As a life's mission.

5. Let go: Finding your purpose can be a tiring treadmill of self-questioning. Maybe take a few months off worrying about that and get back to having some fun.

JUDGEMENTS THAT BREED JOY

"Peace begins with a smile."

— Mother Teresa

I believe that most of us, if we were honest with ourselves, find it really difficult to remain totally non-judgemental of others. Millions of years of evolution have given us a quite incredible tool in terms of the human body. A mind-blowingly effective, inbuilt safety system; one that we don't even need to be consciously aware of and that works whether we think we need it or not. It is so quick at reacting to what it has perceived as a threat, or to be unsafe, that it's already jumped into action before we think we need to turn it on or engage it. The system uses our key human senses; sight, sound, touch, smell and taste, as well as hunger, thirst, proprioception and equilibrioception or, roughly speaking, balance. The body and brain make billions of calculations daily to work out whether something or someone is safe or dangerous. Whether we like it or not, we are subconsciously using our judgment to work out whether we are hypothetically or actually safe with this person or in this situation, or not.

Even whilst listening to someone's voice, we are making micro-judgments of their speech pattern and prosody (pitch, volume, tempo and rhythm) to ascertain whether they are a possible threat to us either physically, intellectually or psychologically. Arguably, when getting to know someone for the first time, it's often less important what people say, rather than how it is said. The body and brain use all available inputs to make a decision; which we will become aware of as a conscious, but often indescribable, feeling such as love at first sight. We've no doubt all experienced it! Yet this initial judgment, clever as it is, is not always 100% accurate or right.

Many of our judgments are based on past experiences. In trying to protect us, the brain will store what it considers useful memories – usually the less favourable ones – to keep us safe. It uses those painful experiences to guard us against future risk or threat so it will often err on the side of safety and be reluctant to openly engage. Would you discuss all of your fears and mistakes with a total stranger in the same way you would open up to a best friend? It's unlikely.

Fortunately, with a flexible attitude, self-awareness and active practice, we can learn to change perspective. We can preload these often-subconscious judgments, by learning to remember the good times and positive experiences; considering people or situations as a challenge that floods positive stress hormones such as dopamine into the body, rather than as a threat. That's what we call being optimistic. A positive mindset or positive mental attitude. Seeing the glass as half full rather than half empty. This changes the way our body, and brain, may interpret what it is looking at; considering it a potential opportunity to learn something new and even to grow as a result. Judgments that breed joy are conscious reflections of who we are and appreciation of life in general. It's something we often overlook when comparing ourselves to others we consider more fortunate than ourselves.

'Comparison is the thief of joy.'
– Theodore Roosevelt

Having an optimistic outlook on life is a key factor in maintaining personal resilience by empowering us to face the uncertainties of life head-on. With an understanding that good and bad experiences will happen to us all, appreciating life for what it is and learning to adapt along the way, affords us an opportunity to alter our mindset and live a meaningful, fulfilling and enjoyable life.

'Do not complain about growing old, it is a privilege denied to many.'
– Mark Twain

Coaching Questions

1. Smiles: Name three things that make you smile.

2. Advice: What one piece of advice would you offer a newborn child?

3. Alive: At what time in your recent past have you felt most passionate and alive?

4. Active: How often do you exercise?

5. Happier: If you could do one thing to make yourself feel happier, what would it be?

A 2019 analysis of 69,744 NHS nurses and 1,429 men from the Normative Aging Study suggested that **optimism is specifically related to 11 to 15% longer life span and to greater odds of achieving "exceptional longevity"** (live to over 85 years).

Habituators

1. Shine: Sunlight (by releasing Vitamin D) and exercise release the hormone serotonin, which is great for improving mood, creating feelings of happiness and well-being.

2. Reflect: Meditation, regular exercise, laughter (and/or crying), eating spicy food all release endorphins; the hormones that are produced by the body to relieve stress, pain, anxiety and depression.

3. Move: Regular exercise, goal setting (especially long-term), practising mindfulness, being creative (playing music or writing a book) release the hormone dopamine, which gives us drive, determination, learning, pleasure and importantly, enables us to think and plan.

4. Interact: Social connection, exercise, listening to music and physical touch all release oxytocin (the so-called love hormone) which encourages us to bond, trust and build meaningful relationships.

5. Daily: Do a little bit of the above each day to be happy and joyful.

*'Optimism is associated with exceptional longevity in two epidemiologic cohorts of men and women', Proceedings of the National Academy of Sciences of the United States of America (2019)

K

KILLING WITH KINDNESS

"Every time you solve someone's problems or give them advice or an answer to their elusive question... you are denying them an opportunity to learn and develop for themselves."

— Anonymous

There is the age-old belief that too much of a good thing can be bad for us. Well it turns out to be pretty accurate, too. The body naturally produces hormones that make us feel happy and rewarded for achieving things during the process of living and it helps motivate us to do it again. But here's the thing; if we have too much of a good thing, we can become desensitised by what's known as overstimulation. This is when the positive or 'happy' hormones are kept at a high level and not allowed to fall and naturally recover. This often happens with addictions to things that offer instant gratification; such as gaming, using social media or excessive fast food consumption. So, limiting these types of activities is really important in maintaining a balanced lifestyle.

'Be kind' is an age old mantra, which finds new gravitas, particularly within the new age troll-riddled online community. We, well most of us, know that being kind to others is good for us all. It is proven to be crucial for maintaining personal resilience and human connection. So why wouldn't you be kind? Often, the person we are least kind to is ourselves. Negative self-talk can scupper personal or team performance. But perhaps there is a balance to consider and a question always worth asking before intervening and helping: 'Is this act of kindness that's being offered actually going to help the one in need?'

Human kindness may be the greatest gift we can bestow, and so I am in no-way suggesting being deliberately unkind to someone or discard compassion. It is only right that if someone is physically or psychologically injured or ill, then they should receive the necessary and suitable love and support available to them, but sometimes in our rush to help someone in need, including ourselves, we are potentially hindering them/ourselves in facing future challenges. In Chapter 7 we cover human growth and the fact that we as humans need to struggle at times in order to develop strategies to help ourselves recover, rather than automatically wait for someone to come and pick us up; potentially initiating a maladaptive form of co-dependency or learned helplessness. This approach again needs careful balance and deliberation. Sometimes a simple hug is all we need, sometimes it is not.

But sometimes, for some, life can be tough, really tough especially in these COVID times. And when we are in the depths of despair, or feeling totally overwhelmed by a situation, the body does a curious thing; it jettisons our ability to think straight. For us sophisticated inhabitants of the 21st century this seemingly makes little sense; 'Er, hello brain? I need to think my way out of this situation now, please'. But this biological and physiological reaction is a remnant from primitive times, when an emergency was more likely to involve, a physical threat such as from a bear or wolf perhaps. At which point, the body's top priority was physicality; to either run away or throw a spear, so mental reasoning was shut down. Today, thankfully, most of us aren't often in frequent life-or-death encounters in our daily lives (although some clearly are such as the emergency services and some of the military, etc). So it may feel extreme when our brain's ancient fight or flight mode kicks in after a particularly stressful time at work or home. But psychological overwhelm can happen to any of us and so at times we all may need the support of others. However, to avoid 'killing-with-kindness', I believe, it needs to be a carefully considered response, with a 'what next?' approach.

In a performance setting, we will all struggle at times, it's part of the package. In aiming high we are putting ourselves at potential risk of failing and so we should look to develop strategies that enable us to learn from those situations, accept what has happened and move on. If we don't work out personal ways to get through setbacks or heartbreak then we stand the risk of becoming stuck, which in due course may prevent progression. The important thing is that we work out ways to avoid becoming overwhelmed (where possible) which requires awareness of what's going on inside and around us. It is during these tough times we all need to try and maintain flexible thinking patterns; to find ways to switch back on, by using techniques such as diaphragmatic breathing to disengage the fight-or-flight mode.

As a performance coach, I have learned to try and explore all options available to someone, especially when they are regularly facing potential adversity, whether that's with or without support from others. If we, as the coach, or the concerned friend or colleague, want to help those in need then the offer of support is the first step. Just knowing that emotional support is available or even that someone else even cares, can be enough to help someone struck down by grief after losing a loved one, to find a way to pick themselves up and take the first steps to recovery, acceptance and/or safety. Helping others realise that they may already possess many of the attributes they need to deal with adversity and move forward, will build confidence in their own ability to overcome setbacks and maintain resilience in challenging, often stressful times. That way, you may be helping someone to grow rather than potentially 'killing them with kindness'.

"As I look back on my life, I realise that every time I thought I was being rejected from something good, I was actually being re-directed to something better."

—Anonymous

Coaching Questions

1. Kind: Is this action of kindness going to help me or the other person learn for themselves?

2. Export: How does being kind to myself impact others?

3. List: Name five ways to be kind to yourself.

4. Coach: Next time you feel like jumping in to help someone, ask the question: 'What do you think is the best way that I can help you help yourself?'

5. Create: What other ways are there to help someone?

Habituators

1. Random: Do one act of random kindness per day.

2. Recall: Acknowledge one of your own achievements each day (even a small one).

3. Think: Each day remember something that made you feel good about yourself.

4. Own: You are the best expert about yourself.

5. Grin: Smile. Smiling has a positive impact on ourselves and others.

LATENCY – DISCOVERING WHAT YOU ARE MADE OF

"Potential is a priceless treasure. All of us have gold hidden within, but we have to dig to get it out."

— Joyce Meyer

Imagine having something within us that we don't yet know about. Or finding that there is a new ceiling to our already acknowledged skill set. Quite simply, latency is the state of existing but not yet being developed; a concealment of our true potential. Our true potential can be both thrilling and terrifying in equal measure. Let's explore some strategies and see if we can discover what we are truly made of.

There are a couple of things that can trip us up and prevent us from unlocking this latency and understanding them is helpful in overcoming them. Firstly, as Stephen King once wrote: 'Fear can hold you prisoner, hope can set you free.' I guess we can all recognise a situation where someone would rather not try, and fail, than give it everything they've got and fail. This self-sabotage will not help us unlock our potential. Whilst stepping into the unknown can be terrifying, it can also be hugely rewarding. I was never a volleyball player (I'm only 5ft 2ins "tall"), nor was I a canoeist, yet stepping up to both these challenges unlocked potential in me and consequently led to opportunities I could never have imagined.

It would have been easy to retire immediately upon crossing the finish line in Rio 2016, with the gold medal tucked in my pocket. Plenty of athletes do when they reach this pinnacle. I could have retired unbeaten. I could have retired at the top of my game with no fear of losing that status. But retiring then would have meant I never knew how fast we could actually make the boat. In truth, the thought of retiring could have been tempting, but the thought of being bold, brave and seeing what we could achieve was more enticing.

Many people never really look inside themselves to see what's there. Our aversion to fear can keep us from ever really putting ourselves in a truly challenging situation. By understanding the process of performance, I knew I had more to give but I didn't know if this would pay off. Would trying and failing mean my past achievements meant less? Or would not trying and never knowing what we could have achieved be worse? It's a balancing act of risk vs. reward. Two of my values are challenge and passion; both within my control and both fundamental to how I behave. So whilst acknowledging the incredible situation I found myself in, I wanted to see what else was possible. I wasn't done yet.

The second potential blocker is a tendency to experience Imposter Syndrome. This is a psychological pattern in which we doubts our accomplishments and has a persistent internalised fear of being exposed as a fraud. At times in my career I've experienced this, attributing a good performance to luck, a fluke or a big tailwind. If I let these thoughts stagnate it would, of course, prevent me unlocking my true potential. However, grounding ourselves in a clear understanding of our values and the behaviours they produce will ensure we make decisions based on careful thought and strategy. Acknowledging what we have achieved (and crucially, why or how) is an important step to allow us to move on and be open to what is still to be discovered within us.

We now understand two things that can impact us and keep us locked in latency. It is also important to recognise that we don't have to always take every opportunity. The power comes in questioning ourselves to ensure we are applying rational thinking to each opportunity. The grass isn't always greener. Allowing ourselves to stay in what could be considered a latent period, where we don't endlessly seek to develop or progress, may, in fact, be just what we need. It could be a little oasis for a period of time where we allow ourselves more reflection, more time to gain a balance and more time to think, thus promoting better decisions in the future. The important thing to remember is that if we take an opportunity to unlock our potential and it doesn't quite pan out, we evaluate the situation to ensure it doesn't inhibit future attempts to discover our true potential. We can ask ourselves honestly: 'Was it the right situation?' 'Was it the right time for me?' 'Did I do everything I could have?' 'Is the outcome or success under my control?' Simply taking some time to assess can help ensure we keep a can-do attitude and that we empower ourselves by learning. That will be the difference in steering our drive and desire towards the next goal or opportunity.

Sometimes a period of latency could be exactly what we need. Have you ever thought: 'I'd love to do that but I don't have the time.' Or: 'I don't have the energy to do that?' Simply taking a time out and acknowledging what we have is a hugely beneficial process. Being grateful and recognising what we have achieved and how we have done it can help us make sound decisions in the moment as to what to pursue next. Equally, it can help identify areas where we might find new heights to our existing talents. An injury provided me with a period of latency. One that I didn't want. One that derailed my progress towards my goals. But equally it was one that was crucial in getting a better understanding of my own mental health and allowed me the time to develop better, more resilient strategies to cope with the demands of a high performance environment.

It also allowed us to focus on areas that we would usually ignore, the hard-to-reach small performance gains that take time to realise. It is possible that coming through a period of latency is actually a hugely powerful moment of learning that we should consider taking into our next ambitious drive for performance, refocused and with our batteries recharged.

So, whatever your gold medal may be, ask yourselves the following questions to ensure you make an informed decision to allow you to unlock your potential and leave latency behind.

Coaching Questions

1. Reflect: Are you in a period of latency or not? Do you need to have a fallow period?

2. Refocus: Do you need a period of latency to recharge, refocus and reassess?

3. Explore: Does this possible challenge excite you?

4. Internalise: Do you want to do this? Shall we go there? Trust your gut feeling.

5. Evaluate: Have you evaluated performances that haven't worked out as you wanted accurately enough? Failure to do this may result in more periods of latency as we fear failure again.

Habituators

1. Discover: Find the opportunity. Without trying and sometimes failing we might never know our true potential.

2. Courage: Be bold and be brave. Doing the same thing because it's always worked will rarely push us to our true potential.

3. Squeeze: Is the juice worth the squeeze? Do you believe you can do everything it takes to give you the best chance of success?

4. Meta: Ask yourself if you will regret not stepping out of your comfort zone.

5. Schedule: Plan in a short period of latency and brain-and-body holiday. Some quality self-care time where you don't have to seek more, pursue everything and tirelessly go after self-improvement. Sometimes this time gives us more learnings and more gains than relentlessly trucking on.

A study by a Professor Hal E. Hershfield from the Kellogg School of Management, Northwestern University, conducted a study in which virtual reality was used to allow some subjects to look at digitally aged versions of themselves. They were then asked how they would spend $1,000 across a range of catergories. **Those who saw their potential future chose to invest twice as much in a retirement account as those who didn't** see their digitally aged self.

V

MOTIVATION AND MOOD MUSIC

"By definition, you have to live until you die. Better to make that life as complete and enjoyable an experience as possible, in case death is shite, which I suspect it will be."

— Irvine Welsh, *Trainspotting*

Here's a question: What's the mood music in our lives? Hotels choose very carefully the background music for lobbies and elevators. They design an audiosphere; a sound world, to impact and influence the emotions and motivations of their customers. The highest performers across many spheres of life take control of their mood music and motivations. In working with these high performers one insight stands out; motivation comes and goes. Weird, that. Across business, sport, music, the arts... motivation comes and goes. One of the highest performers in our team, running one of our biggest international leadership projects, told me yesterday: 'It's not really doing it for me anymore.' Wow. David Cameron famously compared his faith to radio reception in the Cotswolds: 'It sort of comes and goes'. Motivation is similar. Nobody wakes up motivated every day. And if we compare ourselves to these ephemeral, imaginary superhumans we will never measure up. Our research shows that people who appear super-motivated, and consistently motivated, have a variety of subskills that give this illusion of constant positivity and go-get-it. Yet, unlike a desert mirage, this illusion is not based on a false image. These motivated people are merely covering the gaps on a bad day, leaving those around them with the appearance of consistent high motivation. Covering the gaps on a bad day is easy, if there aren't too many bad days. So, these people are also managing their lives such that most days are a good day. Turn up the mood music, people. Managing our work so that most days are a good day involves taking proactive steps to build as much of the life that we want, as we can. It means being

proactive about relationships, our work, building skills, building strength, endurance and resilience. They say a journey of a thousand miles starts with a single step. But if you were to race a thousand miles, the journey starts way before the single step. With training, preparation, support team, equipment, and more.

Motivation is a precious resource, and also a consumable resource. Designing a life, that, at the end of each day, leaves us energised, grateful, happy, rested... this is how to create a surplus of motivation. The elite performers across all spheres recognise that, if each day leaves us a tiny bit more depleted, eventually our motivations will decrease. However, life is also an unfolding adventure, with ups and downs and what motivated us last month, might not motivate us next month. Human beings require challenge. If we get used to something, adapt to it, the challenge decreases. For example, a teacher with limited experience can be excellent, despite lack of skills, but someone with more experience and deeper skills may perform worse. An athlete with a track record of success may become stale. A CEO with years at the top may lose their mojo. Discipline is a core muscle linked to motivation. People with high levels of discipline are able to execute without mental effort. Without tapping in to motivation. It just happens. Much of our lives can be run on solid disciplines. From making our bed, to being on time, to being proactive in sales, or remembering to send a text to say thanks to a team mate. None of this requires motivation if it's a highly valued discipline. So, we could ask: What can be programmed into disciplined routines? What am I wasting my precious resources of motivation on? Those that achieve high performance run much of their lives in routines, habits and disciplines, and save their motivation for the tough stuff, the big push, the tricky time, game day, end of quarter, a battle. To put it another way: when the going gets tough, the tough get going.

Motivational leaks are like running a bath without the plug in. Once plugged, the bath can fill up pretty fast. It can fill to overflow. Fulfilment is the end result of motivation, applied, without leaks. Fulfilment is the payoff of hard work, dealing with issues, putting in 100% consistently, holding high standards. Often, people we see as motivated are actually just fulfilled. When you are fulfilled, hard work becomes easier. And the mood music of your life is up-tempo. In working with global organisations and developing leaders we pay careful attention to the source of motivation. Are people internally motivated?It's what psychologists call intrinsic motivation. Or are they externally motivated by extrinsic factors?

	Motivation	Goals
Intrinsic	You do the activity because it's internally rewarding. You may do it because it's fun, enjoyable and satisfying.	Goals come from within and the outcomes satisfy your basic psychological needs for autonomy, competence, and relatedness.
Extrinsic	You do the activity in order to get an external reward in return.	Goals are focused on an outcome and don't satisfy your basic psychological needs. Goals involve external gains, such as money, fame, power or avoiding consequences.

Here are some examples of intrinsic motivation:

- Participating in a sport because it's fun and you enjoy it rather than doing it to win an award
- Learning a new language because you like experiencing new things, not because your job requires it
- Spending time with someone because you enjoy their company and not because they can further your social standing
- Exercising because you enjoy physically challenging your body instead of doing it to lose weight or fit into an outfit
- Volunteering because you feel content and fulfilled rather than needing it to meet a school or work requirement
- Going for a run because you find it relaxing or are trying to beat a personal record, not to win a competition
- Taking on more responsibility at work because you enjoy being challenged and feeling accomplished, rather than to get a raise or promotion

Those of us who work in the world of motivation know that, if we can find ways to tap into our own or others' intrinsic motivations, we harness an unlimited source that is persistent, long-lasting and self-sustaining. When we try to use external motivators, we create a cycle of dependency that, whilst it may produce short-term payoffs, requires constant attention and feeding. An example of the weakness of external motivation is Premier League football. It's often the case that big money transfers flop. Once they become the £100 million-pound player they dreamed of, they no longer have the motivation of striving to become the £100 million-pound player. The same is true of business execs. I've seen many people reach their external goals, only to realise they have lost their drive because it was just external motivation, which once achieved, disappears.

The most successful strategy is to set up our life patterns based on what genuinely motivates us, rather than working out how to bribe ourselves or others.

Coaching Questions

1. Explore: What motivates you? Why?

2. Source: Are you normally in a pattern of intrinsic or extrinsic motivation?

3. Success: To what extent is success an inner feeling or an outer achievement?

4. Reflect: What did you find out about yourself during the toughest times in your life?

5. Leaks: Where are you leaking motivation? How can you plug the gaps?

Habituators

1. Review your goals: Focus on your intrinsic motivators. Refocus your goals on what you are intrinsically motivated to do.

2. Intention: Set an intention for each day. At the start of the day think about your motivators. Try to mentally connect your efforts to your purpose.

3. Interview: Who do you know who is really motivated? Interview three people about what drives them.

4. Audit: Write a list of motivational leaks. Address one of them. Then another. Then another.

5. Escape: New motivation comes from rest and escape. Take a holiday. Take a break. Be open to what emerges in these seasons.

NUGATORY, NOISE AND NO

"It isn't the mountains ahead to climb that wear you out; it's the pebble in your shoe."

— Muhammed Ali

Ali's quotation suggests that small things can make a big difference in life. Perhaps in coaching this is why we take time to explore the current situation: 'What's happening here?' or: 'Is there a pebble in my shoe?' Getting into the real nitty-gritty before taking those initial small steps forward on a journey is vital, but there are a few ever-present factors that are often overlooked or taken for granted.

As humans, we all have a limited capacity in terms of accessible personal resources, such as brain power, strength and motivation. This is why we need to be selective in considering what is important to us and what isn't, before choosing how much time and effort to invest in the things we really want to achieve. Small things do matter. The following seemingly innocuous, words are worth at least thinking about.

Nugatory work (adjective, 'of no value or importance').This is all about doing something for no reason, apart from the fact that it's what's been done previously or it's what's expected. It's like reading a lengthy document on a subject which holds little personal interest or value or spending longer at work than we need to just because it's what we perhaps think is expected. Beware; this does not mean that I don't like doing things simply because I don't think that I will need or use them. It's more about having made a personal judgment call on

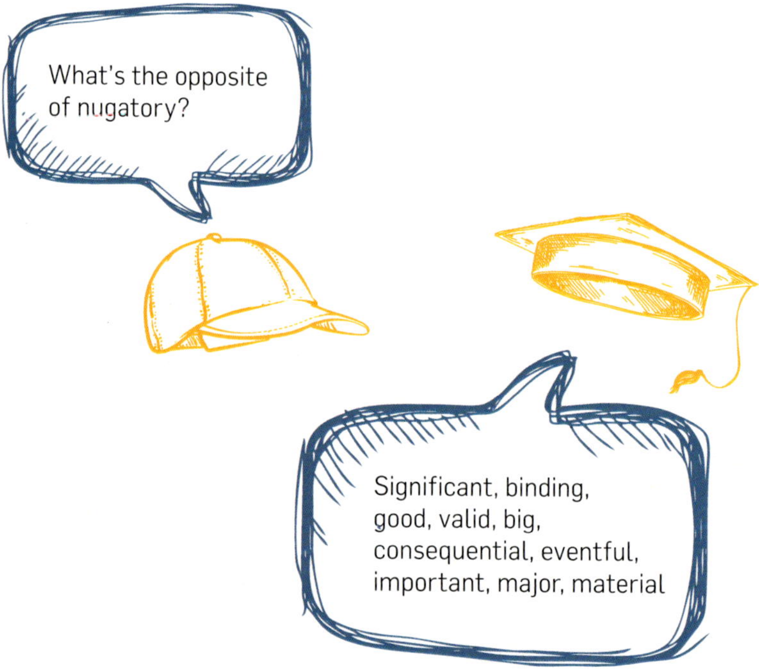

whether what I'm doing is useful or has purpose to me or the team. Much of my former military career was spent preparing for things that seldom actually happened. These were known as drills or SOPs (Standard Operating Procedures). Whether shooting, driving or parachuting, hours of practice drills were conducted for the just-in-case. Not just thinking about, or talking about, but physically doing. Your weapon jamming when firing or your parachute failing to open correctly. Many of these things didn't ever occur, or rarely happened at most.

However, having the knowledge of what you should do in those situations improves, at the very least, your technical skill levels and it increases your confidence in your ability to look after yourself and your colleagues, if the worst were to happen. I would not consider these types of drills as nugatory work. On the contrary; through diligent and exhaustive repetition, these skills became second nature; subconsciously filed away so that the brain doesn't have to employ unnecessary time and effort to consciously recall them; like riding a bike or driving. In coaching, it's known as moving from being consciously competent, where we are aware of a skill but are not yet proficient, to unconsciously competent, where performing the skill becomes automatic.

While nugatory effort requires conscious consideration in order to recognise, mitigate and avoid, noise is usually just there in the background and its effects are often overlooked. That familiar reassuring sound that makes you feel warm or complete or a constant tick or irritation that makes you feel on edge. I distinctly remember a colleague who was chewing gum so loudly it severely affected my concentration until one day I felt compelled to say sometime to him. Noise, as with our nugatory efforts, is often there using up valuable unconscious capacity.

Emma knows all about creating boundaries around noise – from harnessing the crowd's deafening support to achieve greatness at the Rio Olympics, to not letting our own internal noise distract us. I'll let Emma explain...

'They look good.' 'Check them out, I bet they're fast.' 'I can't beat them.' All thoughts that have gone through my mind pre-race and there is nothing more frustrating for a coach than an athlete sharing these uncontrollables, these noises. I hadn't ever really considered the impact of paying attention to noise until I learned not to. Often our moment to perform is exactly that, a moment, whether it be sport, business or whatever we need to be ready for that moment if we want to give our best performance. Like many things, dealing with noise is a skill. We can't simply ignore it and pretend we didn't see the huge athlete on the start line next to us, or that we didn't feel the side wind, that we know is from our worst side.

More importantly we need to recognise it, accept it, and remind ourselves of our plan to deliver that performance; control the controllables; scenario planning/cue cards/questions/practice.' – Emma

Noise can also be tangible when you think of it as clutter. Over the years to deal with things as they crop up. After nights in the arctic, jungle or desert I learned very quickly to only unpack what is needed, be it cooker, sleeping bag, perhaps dry clothes. Then, after I'd used it or completed my task, I'd pack it away. That way, I'd always know where things were when I needed them next and it meant that I wouldn't have to do it later. This is particularly important when we're tired, cold and wet and our functional and cognitive skills start to deteriorate. Some people can choose to be discerning and tidy and proactively sort out their kit or desk. Others, choose not to and lose precious time, focus and energy in managing chaos ... often when they least need it!

As a performance coach, where I support others in managing transition and changes in life, I've noticed that many people try to control things that have no control over, and yet neglect the things that they can control.

Maintaining some form of functional skill has, I'm sure, helped me manage and mitigate setbacks and potential traumas faced over the years. Not allowing noise or clutter to become overwhelming has been a key part of me managing my life performance.

Interference and distraction can be both negative and positive and setting boundaries of what can interfere with us is a fundamental performance skill for a person, a team, a company. Which brings us to 'no'.

'It's only by saying no that you can concentrate on the things that are really important' – Steve Jobs

No. We can always say: 'no'. More times than perhaps we think. It's a hugely powerful word, often discounted as having any positive value. The secret is to give it some thought and remember that every choice we make is linked to a set of consequences, good or bad.

Imagine you are in a plane, about to do a parachute jump. You have your equipment on and are sitting on the floor as the plane climbs to an altitude of 12,000ft, where you will be invited to an open door. Once there, you will be expected to throw yourself out into the slip stream of fast air, and plummet towards earth for fifty or so seconds at around 120mph. Enveloped by the dull drone of the aircraft engines, you feel surprisingly calm and relatively relaxed, as is the general atmosphere amongst you and the other jumpers.

You reach 12,000ft. The door is pulled open by the jump master and instantly the inside of the aircraft is hit with a rush of freezing air and deafening noise. Your mind is now racing and your heart pumping. You struggle to get that breath and you desperately try to remember all of the drills you spent days rehearsing in the framed harnesses in the aircraft hangar. Drills, practised over and over again. Drills that you probably thought were a complete waste of time (more people die getting knocked off their bike than die in parachuting accidents). But now those drills are suddenly so relevant and undoubtedly needed. It quickly dawns on you; 'I don't have to jump. I can always say "no."'

But in a moment of clarity, you remember that you chose to be there. You chose to put yourself in that position. Surrounded by the natural noise of the experience. The excitement (and fear) of others, doing something that you spent months, if not years, looking forward to. Hours of practice and seemingly needless, rehearsals of sitting in uncomfortable swings getting ready for this moment.

What about the others? What about me? How will I live this down?

You can always say 'no'...but in this instance you choose to say 'yes'...and have the flight of your life.

In coaching, when a client becomes stuck, or is seemingly unwilling to change or move, we often go back to the start and ask the questions: 'Is doing nothing an option?' 'What would happen if you did nothing?' 'What would happen if you said "no"?' As long as whatever decision you make is a conscious one, either to stop the nugatory stuff, acknowledge the noise and do nothing, or say 'no', then it's a positive choice and can be a really powerful message to yourself.

Coaching Questions

1. Chore: Am I going through the motions or is there a point to this action?

2. Interference: What noise am I hearing? Is it useful or do I need to ignore it?

3. Self: What noise am I making? Is it a noise that I want others to be hearing?

4. Consequences: What are the consequences of me saying 'no'?

5. Inaction: Is doing nothing an option?

Habituators

1. Pause: Take a moment to think whether what you're doing is real and has relevance.

2. Stop: At least once a day stop and listen. What can you hear?

3. Hesitate: Before you jump in and say 'yes' to something that you don't really want to do, or say 'no' to something that you really do want to do, take a moment to consider the consequences. Then make an informed decision.

4. Focus: Remember that you know yourself better than anyone.

5. Here's a quote: 'This above all: to thine own self be true, and it must follow, as the night the day, thou canst not then be false to any man.'

Scientists at the Princeton University Neuroscience Institute have used fMRI and other approaches to show that our brains like order so much that **constant visual reminders of disorganisation drain our cognitive resources and reduce our ability to focus.**

The study, in which 346 young adults completed self-reported measures of procrastination, self-identification with possessions, clutter, place attachment, and psychological home – found that when participants cleared clutter from their work environment, they were better able to focus and process information, and their productivity increased.

Procrastinators and Clutter: An Ecological View of Living with Excessive "Stuff" (2018)

OWNERSHIP, ORIGINATION AND ORGANISING

"Do your thing. Do it unapologetically. Don't be discouraged by criticism. You probably already know what they're going to say. Pay no mind to the fear of failure. It's far more valuable than success. Take ownership, take changes, and have fun. And no matter what, don't ever stop doing your thing."

— Asher Roth

Here's a game I like to play. It's called Bums. Get a few friends. Make a circle. Find a football. The rules are simple. One touch. One bounce. The aim is to keep the ball under control using soccer skills. At any given point you are only allowed one touch. The ball must only bounce once between touches. Each player has four lives, and when you have used up your four lives (B, U, M, S) you must kneel down and each of the remaining team gets to take a penalty – and try to hit you in the bum.

Playing this game throws up some fascinating human behavior. Blame. And ownership. Because when it goes wrong in life (or in Bums), whose fault is it? In my company, and most of my life, I practice maximum ownership. If anything goes wrong it's my fault. If anything needs owning, I will own it. If I pass by an accident I will stop, and go and see if I can help. Even if there is a crowd. Because maybe the crowd isn't owning the situation. Maybe they are just spectating. Maybe they are not an aged boy scout trained in first aid. I should not assume that there is one person in a crowd of 20 that is trained in CPR. The bystander effect was first recognised by social psychologists John M. Darley and Bibb Latané in 1968 following the murder of Kitty Genovese. Kitty was stabbed repeatedly by a stranger on her way home one night. She staggered screaming through her neighbourhood for hours, and ultimately, dying; despite there being dozens of onlookers from apartment windows. Every single individual assumed someone else had called the police. It's a sobering realisation that, the bigger the crowd, the less we see ownership. Conversely, it just takes a single individual to extend themselves and own more, and the whole situation might be different.

In Bums there is often a discussion about who should lose a life. Is it the person who passed the ball? Or the one who failed to reach the ball?

Devilishly, I always put my hand up and say that I will lose my life. I've seen in every game of Bums I've ever played that this consistent ownership mindset utterly changes the game. It only takes one person to take ownership, and do it loudly, and consistently. And then... transformation. Instead of blame and catching people out, it galvanises a team. It makes people start taking responsibility. It makes them sprint faster, jump higher, smile more, laugh harder. It turns combative blaming 'It wasn't my fault!' into 'I don't mind, I'll take it'. What have you got to lose if you will take the punishment anyway? When building teams in businesses and working with leaders, ownership is at the heart of the commitment it takes to build high performance. Take ownership. What have you got to lose? Take ownership over and above what's required. It can start with one person. And spread like wildfire. The opposite of ownership is abdication. Renouncing the throne. Failing to fulfil a responsibility. It's obvious that lack of commitment cannot be at the core of high performance and outstanding results. An elite mindset is high on ownership, low on abdication. High on commitment, low on giving up. High on stepping up, low on stepping out. High on serving the group. Low on saying: 'It's not fair.' To work on this is simple. Start putting your hand up. Start saying: 'I'll own that.' It could be the hoovering at home. Or a personal favourite: cleaning the work kitchen. Proofreading a document. Delivering tricky feedback. Take ownership. We will see the transformation in ourselves and others.

Ownership is at the heart of building teams. Many, many leaders get this wrong, focusing on themselves. Driving ownership is probably one of the most incredible things a leader can do. Whilst working with Airbus I've been privileged to get to know a few of the Flight Physics team. For a two-year period their manager went on sabbatical and they became a Self-Organised Team. As part of an experiment for their organisation they shared out every part of management amongst the team and created systems and protocols to make joint decisions. Being physicists, they created a logical formula and an equation: 'Every person is an element of the intersection of responsibility and autonomy.' That's the definition of ownership. Autonomous responsibility. A self-organising team combines each individual's knowledge and skills with the multiplier of attitude.

What was telling about their presentation was that ownership dripped off them. They could explain how they had tackled every challenge, without giving up, together. They had worked around every obstacle. Faced every difficulty. Ownership oozed from their every pore.

The highest human performers take full ownership and responsibility. They don't need managers. They can work autonomously. Those interested in building the highest performing teams seek out such individuals. Often, they are humble, simple people. Who just won't quit. Who can handle responsibility. Who are the first to put their hand up when things go wrong.

$$\forall \text{ person } E \left[\text{Responsible}\right] \cap \left[\text{Autonomous}\right]$$

$$\text{Team} = \left(\text{Knowledge} + \text{Skills}\right) \cdot \text{Attitude}$$

Coaching Questions

1. Own: What do you currently own? What do you *really* own?

2. Assess: Where are you abdicating?

3. Admit: How easy and how quickly can you admit mistakes and make apologies?

4. Grasp: What would greater ownership look like in your life? (Maybe take a look again at the balance wheel.)

5. Learn: Who exemplifies ownership that you can learn from?

Habituators

1. Commitment: Review your commitments to work, family, hobbies etc. Decide on your priority commitments. Rationalise the rest.

2. Responsibility: Try taking more responsibility for the small things. Tidy care. Clean shoes. Putting out the bins. What is the impact?

3. Autonomy: Take some actions (morally acceptable ones) that would normally require permission, without permission. What happens?

4. Team: Put together a team for a project based on ownership.

5. Sorry: Who should you apologise to? Write a list. Get it done.

The Journal of Engineering Design outlines 'routes' to ownership through a bidirectional model (pictured) including 'Be Goals' which reflect the desires of an individual (ie. to be in control), 'Do Goals' which are more tangible (ie. control the car), and 'Motor Goals' which are describe how the Do Goal is achieved (ie. Move the steering wheel). Do Goals are mapped to the routes to psychological ownership: control, intimate knowledge and self-investment.

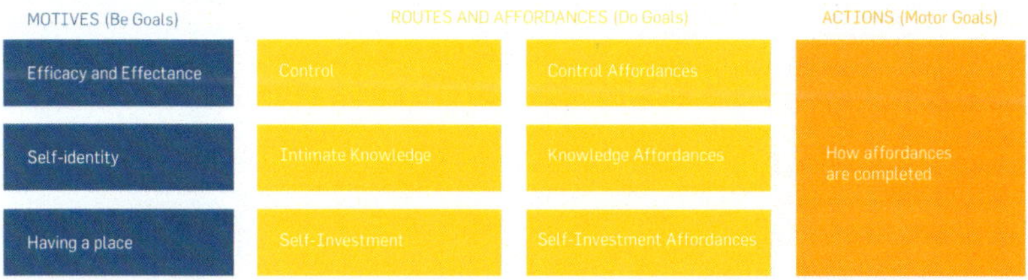

POWERFUL PLANNING AND PRIORITISATION

"Planning is bringing the future into the present, so you can do something about it now."

— Alan Lakein

'Plan the paddle and paddle the plan!' If my 68-year-old mother can realise the potential of planning, we all can. Mum has always been interested in my training and performances, madly waving her flag on the bankside and asking endless questions, but when she sent this message before a race day, it really hit home. I guess the message from the more mature Mrs Wiggs is simple. If you've made a plan, done the work to the best of your ability, then the actual moment of performance takes care of itself. 'If only it was that simple' I hear you say. Well, actually, it is. We can take huge confidence from planning and prioritisation. Because then, potentially, the actual performance becomes more automatic. Less stressful. And as a consequence, more successful.

Fundamental to a successful plan is knowing where you are heading. Having a clear idea of the outcome you seek, whether that's an actual measurable, or a feeling or ideology, is vital. If you don't know where you want to go, how on earth can you make a plan to get there? As the quote at the start of the chapter suggests, planning can bring that future moment into the present – so we can actually do something about it.

Once we know where we want to go (or what we want to achieve) we need to ensure we make a precise plan to get there. This is sometimes the part people miss out. It is crucial to identify what may trip us up along the way or identify our current work-ons that we would need to amend to make the plan more successful. Most will just go ahead, gung-ho style, forging towards their goal whilst missing critical steps or opportunities that could either make their journey easier or, in fact, more successful. And this is where a powerful plan really has an impact.

Understanding the Why, the How and the When of our plan is fundamental to the success of it. Why would you expend energy and precious time on a task if it has no value to your end goal? Ask yourself how high your drive or desire will be for a task that has no understood relevance. The power of a plan is in the questioning and challenging we apply to the process of making it. I see athletes who simply do the plan they are told to do, without questioning or understanding. For some this pays off with lower (perceived) stress levels. But I would suggest for the majority, they are failing to reach their full potential.

The power of establishing our Why, How and Who is crucial and certainly an underused tool in our performance armour. 'Why is this task important?' 'How can I ensure I am in a better place to perform?' 'How can I fit all this into my schedule?' Finally, and potentially most importantly: 'Who can help me?' If we have no plan, we cannot share it with those who may be able to help us. Equally, knowing who or what might hinder our progress will ensure we maximise our chance of success. Knowing who might be that energy-giver when we need it. Who might be the mood-hoover to avoid when we have more important things to focus on. This will not only empower us but leave us with more energy to direct into executing our plan.

Prioritisation is another crucial tool if our planning is to be powerful and successful. We all have the same twenty-four hours in the day. We all have a limit to our available energy and brain capacity. But could we work smarter? Could some simple prioritisation mean we make better use of the resources we have available to us? The process of asking our Why, How and Who will help prioritise. Is answering that email late at night really a priority? Or would switching my brain off, to home mode, be a better use of time to ensure I'm fully rested and recovered for tomorrow? Don't underestimate the power of the switch-off and self-care in delivering our plan. As humans we love to overestimate our capabilities. So keep an eye on what good looks like today. Throw away those to-do lists and instead try writing a today-I-have-time-to list this is hugely empowering as there is nothing more soul-destroying than the never-shortening to-do list.

Within my sport, planning plays a massive role in making the boat go faster. I love to plan, adapt and plan again. I thrive from knowing why we are doing what we are doing and I have found new advantages to building a strong team of who can help me. An important aspect of the planning process is to be ready to adapt and always be prepared to check and challenge. If we don't

feel comfortable doing this we could be missing out on making small but influential changes that could help us reach those performance heights. Questioning and positivity-challenging doesn't need to be confrontational. I have always been known as the questioner. My teammates will roll their eyes as I ask endless questions in meetings and, at times, this presents a challenge. For example: 'I think we should be doing more' could seem quite negative, as if I'm questioning my team's plan and expertise. By slightly changing the words I use I've found an immediate difference in people's responses. 'I think we could be doing more' is suggesting we relook at the plan and seek other opportunities to be better. Changing 'should' for 'could' was far less confrontational to my team and led to much more powerful conversations which, in turn, have impacted my performance.

While preparing for a Paralympic Games we spend every day planning what we will do to get to the games. What it might be like? How we will execute our delivery? Who can help us? Then when you get to the actual Games your plan is to imagine you're at home training where you always train and delivering how you always did. It's a strange conundrum but also an important lesson. Having a plan is vital, adapting that plan is critical. But ultimately, as Mama Wiggs says, 'paddling the plan' is the key.

Coaching Questions

1. **Purpose:** What is your Why?

2. **Process:** Do you have a plan and process for following it?

3. **Communicate:** Does everyone understand the plan?

4. **Flex:** Are you adaptable and able to adjust and alter the plan?

5. **Prioritise:** What are the priorities at each stage of the plan... do these take into account the context you face? e.g. energy levels etc.

Habituators

1. **Have a plan.** You'd be amazed how many people have a goal but not a clear plan.

2. **Share:** Understand the plan and the process to deliver it... who needs to do what and when?

3. **Challenge:** Question the plan as a critical friend, be open to input and challenges that could improve it.

4. **Assess:** Evaluate plan regularly but not too regularly... be objective and open to successes and changes needed.

5. **Check:** Always check and challenge the plan but try swapping 'should' for 'could'.

QUALITY QUESTIONS

"Self-talk is the most powerful form of communication because it either empowers you or it defeats you."
— Anonymous

Self-talk can be the most powerful kind of communication. It can either empower you or defeat you. We must understand our own tendencies of self-talk if we are going to harness its power for our performance. Our own internal dialogue is influenced by our subconscious, and usually our previous experiences. It can reveal our thoughts and our beliefs. The situations in which we find ourselves, create opportunities for self-talk to influence our decisions and our subsequent actions. It can create questions or give us ideas as to the way forward. Therefore it can be a hugely powerful addition to our performance toolbox, if (and this is the key), if we use it correctly.

My own self-talk tends to be quite cautious if the situation is about myself and my performance. It will think: 'What if?' Or throw an immediate question in: 'Are you good enough to beat these people?'. So my initial reactions will define what happens; if I listen to the doubts and feed this angle of self-talk then anxiety and pressure increase. However, if I challenge them with a more positive self-talk conversation, I'm able to answer them with facts. And this normally results in lower anxiety and higher feelings of control, which in turn lead to a set of actions that will facilitate my performance.

There are different types of self-talk which we all favour. Some might lean towards more cautious or negative, some motivational and some instructional. By understanding your own tendencies, you can learn to steer your talk in any direction. Like many aspects of performance, making changes requires consolidated effort and attention. Consequently, most people pay little attention to altering their self-talk tendencies, believing them to be just part of themselves and accepting their chatter. But they're missing out on potential performance gains. I've found using a script helpful in my journey to better understand my self-talk and use it in a positive way. In moments when performance matters, in crucial meetings (or race day, for me), it has proved massively helpful. It is a simple process. Accept the initial feelings or thoughts. Then answer them with questions that require a more rational thought process. Ultimately finishing with the actions you will take.

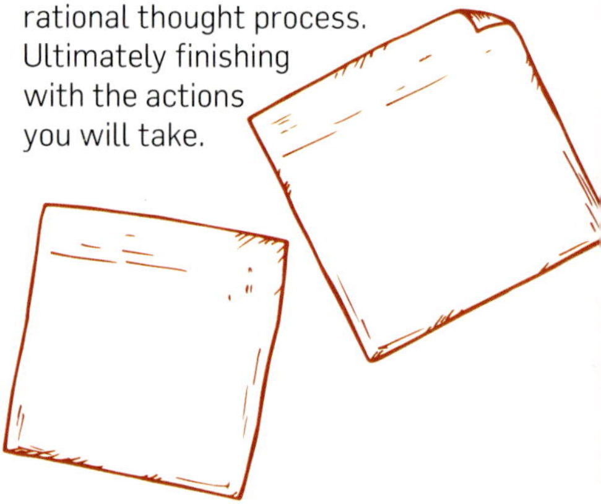

A daily change we can all make to help steer our self-talk is learning to frame the situation; to give it context. It allows us to keep focusing on the process you need to follow to achieve the performance you desire. Failure to do this could lead to unnecessary negative talk ('I should have been better.') which will create stress. Asking yourself: 'What is the context in which I find myself?' and 'What are my expectations, given this context?' will help analyse the outcomes in a more positive way. The best example I can think of is racing in windy conditions. So, imagine the scene; you're 10 days away from a world championship and going through final prep by delivering some time trials....

Race Scenario – Headwind

Your initial aim was to PB, the world champs is days away. You delivered a good, powerful start but it seemed to take forever for the finish line to appear and although you felt powerful it was a battle all the way down. Your technique held strong and you felt connected to the water. Initial self-talk on hearing the time: 'You're kidding, that's rubbish! How can I expect to go to the world champs if I paddle that time? I'll get absolutely smashed. All our training must have been wrong. I haven't done enough. I'm getting worse, not better...'

Without a self-talk conversation where we framed the context before the session, we left ourselves open to negative self-talk. This could, at best, derail our day. And, at worst, drastically impact our confidence levels going forward. By practising our self-talk (it's a skill, like any other, that needs our attention and work), we could have set realistic expectations within our control. And, as a consequence, drawn huge positives from the same situation.

For example: 'Okay, so it's a massive headwind. It's not ideal for fast times but I can't control this. What I need to focus on is delivering my technique with power and strength. It will feel like a long race but I will hold this technique to the end.'

This time, I leave this session feeling pleased with my outcome, given the context. Plus I feel confident that, should there be a headwind again, I have a plan that allows me to deliver the best I can. It is a powerful tool but not an easy one to remember when days are busy and hectic. So I use cue cards to remind me to look at the context and assess myself based on these conditions. Try adding it into your diary or planner as a reminder before big events, This will allow you to make judgments based on what you are facing.

I guess you might be thinking how canoeing in wind relates to you? Well, the scenario may differ but the messaging and process to control our self-talk is the same. So, swap in your own 'performance moment' or a time when you know self-talk has influenced your behaviour, your thoughts or your feelings. And then apply these simple questions....

1. Before, ask yourself: 'What does success look like today?' (consider the context of the situation).

2. After, ask yourself: 'How did I deliver against my goals for today?' 'Could I have done anything better at this moment?'

These two questions will give us a much greater control of our self-talk and help us with a framework on which to set our expectations and review our delivery. Plus, it helps us use helpful rather than damaging questions to guide our self-talk. Allowing us to harness the power within our own heads to help us reach those performance heights.

Coaching Questions

1. Listen: Seek to understand your own self-talk tendencies. What is your go-to in stressful moments?

2. Clarify: Does your self-talk change in different situations or pressures?

3. Focus: Don't ignore your self-talk, but understand you can guide it towards a more useful tool.

4. Script: Write yourself a script of questions to help make changes and direct your self-talk more positively.

5. Embrace: Embrace self-talk. We all do it. Ignoring it won't lead you to the high-performance moments you seek.

The Journal of Applied Sports Psychology published a study on the psychological impact of swimmers' self-talk. The study tracked 44 swimming athletes in two groups –a control group and one group given self-talk* training – and indicated that **self-talk caused an increase in self-compassion levels** and a decrease in competitive anxiety levels.

Habituators

1. Sketch: Set your scene for the day: 'What does good look like today?' This can be influenced by your energy, your schedule, your brain bandwidth, so evaluate yourself on what you have available today.

2. Diagnose: Ask yourself, did you do the best you could, given the situation?

3. Post it: Try placing reminder cards or questions in significant places to help you learn to steer your self-talk in a more performance direction.

4. Accept: Don't expect to stop all your unhelpful talk. Just accept it and then answer it in a rational way (often trying not to do something brings it forwards in our mind and means we do it more).

5. Change: Use your self-talk to bring about small but powerful changes in your everyday life. Recognising when things go well, when you're grateful, or even when you are surprised by your self-talk, can be very positive and helpful going forwards.

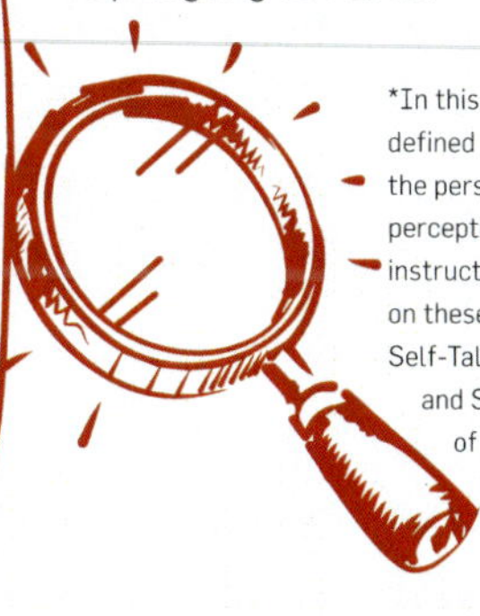

*In this context, self-talk was defined as inner speech in which the person interprets emotions and perceptions and provides themselves instructions and reinforcement based on these. 'The Effects of Motivational Self-Talk on Competitive Anxiety and Self-Compassion' Journal of Applied Sports Psychology (Jan 2017)

RESILIENCE, RESPONSIBILITY AND THE ROUGH STUFF

"Resilience is knowing that you are the only one that has the power and the responsibility to pick yourself up."

— Mary Holloway

We're human, we make mistakes. We sometimes experience unpleasant, even horrible ordeals. And sometimes the proverbial simply hits the fan. In order to move on, we need to find a way of processing our experience; allowing ourselves to try and understand it in some way. To reach a point of acceptance that, what has happened, has happened. In basic terms, we need to figure out a way of dealing with the tough stuff (and that might be really, really tough stuff). Finding a way to learn from the experience and use it to progress in a meaningful way. This is sometimes much easier said than done I appreciate. I lost my Dad on Valentine's Day 2020 and I have given this some considerable thought since. In terms of resilience, Carole Pemberton writes a really useful description: 'Resilience is about being open to learning and growth, being able to take risks because of a sense of being able to deal with the consequences of that risk. Resilience does not protect us from setback, but it ensures we are able to manage our way through it.'

A key point in being resilient lies in the requirement for us to take responsibility for our own lives and experiences. Taking personal responsibility is so important because at any given time, only I (for instance) know what I'm actually thinking and how I'm actually feeling. When making effective changes to my current situation or life in general, I am the only one who will know if those changes are having the desired effects for me. The same goes for all of us.

Personal responsibility and ownership are key facets in terms of human resilience. Having personal awareness of what's

going on inside is a significant factor in establishing personal identity as well as maintaining balance and avoiding personal overwhelm. It is also important when trying to understand our behaviour in a social setting. Sometimes, others can see changes in our behaviour such as irritability, lack of concentration etc. But, quite often, if we take time to reflect and are being honest with ourselves, we notice those changes first. As well as being able to effectively self-regulate (thoughts, feelings, emotions and behaviours), being considered a valued member of a social network can hugely increase a person's sense of worth and personal resilience. Being in a position to adapt your actions to support others, as well as receive support, strengthens essential bonds between groups of people (and many other groups of mammals).

I have a particular interest in working with people that operate in challenging environments; people who voluntarily put themselves in potential harm's way either psychologically or physically for the sake of others. As a result, I have come across many people that are struggling to keep their head above water or have been physically or psychologically injured as a result of what they do.

One thing that I have realised; in order for people to overcome injury, or recover from setbacks most effectively and efficiently, they first need to want to. Fortunately, most of the people I work with have a desire to get back to be the best version of themselves and usually as quickly as they can. That's probably the reason I enjoy coaching so much as people are encouraged to take ownership and responsibility of their situation. Again, attitude is a key force in resilience.

So, if you're thinking of working in challenging environments, such as teaching, law or medicine, be honest with yourself and consider how you're going to look after yourself and how you're going to best support those around you. As with maintaining the ability to endure, resilience can be significantly enhanced through the following:

Exercise:

Am I exercising (or just moving) enough?

Nutrition:

Am I eating a balanced diet? Eat lots of colours!

Sleep:

Am I getting enough, good quality sleep?

Social Support:

Have I got at least one person with whom I can have an honest conversation, apart from myself? Think about organisational as well as individual support.

Having meaningful purpose:

What is my purpose?

Having a positive attitude:

What is my attitude today? Think – Feel – Do, Think – Feel ...
Be proactive. Have a plan. Be prepared. (this needs to work for you).

Before:

What do I need to do to prepare for what I am about to do?

During:

What do I need to do to maintain balance and performance levels in terms of personal strategies that work for me (see Resilience Factors list, above).

After:

What do I need to do to relax, decompress or actively recover? (this does not always mean sitting on the couch with a beer or glass of wine).

From a performance perspective, non-clinical interventions such as coaching can be really effective in helping someone take responsibility and ownership of their issues or concerns. A great coaching tool that can be used equally effectively for others and yourself is OSCAR:

Outcome:

What outcome do I want to achieve?

Situation:

What's the current situation (warts 'n' all)?

Choices and Consequences:

What are my choices? What are the consequences of each choice? (There are always good ones as well as the bad)

Actions:

What actions (from my list of choices) do I need to do to achieve my outcome (small steps, if required)?

Review and / or Reward:

How do I know how I'm progressing? How will I know when I achieve my outcome? How will I reward myself (maybe even just feeling happy with yourself) when I achieve my outcome? Do I deserve that chocolate Wispa?

Think of yourself as the skipper of your own boat (your life). In order to maintain your resilience and deal with the rough seas of life, use your skills, knowledge and positive attitude to keep going even when things get a bit choppy. Having the ability to regulate your thoughts, feelings and behaviours is just like using a boat's resources, such as speed, weight and its trim tabs to keep it on a plane where it runs more smoothly, more efficiently. Making the journey all that more enjoyable.

Coaching Questions

1. **Think:** Where is my attitude at the moment?

2. **Prepare:** Am I prepared for the task that I'm about to undertake?

3. **Bounce:** Have I someone that I can talk to, in all honesty; someone that I can trust? If I can identify one, can I find another?

4. **Enquire:** Ask yourself, why am I doing this? What is my purpose?

5. **Wave:** If I had a magic wand and could grant myself one skill or piece of knowledge that would make me more resilient, what would it be?

Habituators

1. **Confide:** Name one person that you can confide in. Now choose another. Try to have at least five people from different settings that you can talk to, trust and with whom you feel safe. Speak to them individually and ask if they mind being that person should the need arise.

2. **Tools:** Name five things that you need in your resilience toolbox to get by.

3. **Box:** Learn to breathe more effectively. Try box breathing to reduce increased stress levels.

4. **Exhale:** When feeling tense, the first thing you should do is breathe out.

5. **Refresh:** Nature and the fresh air are good for us. Where possible, go for a walk in nature.

A recent working paper from the Center on the Developing Child at Harvard University considers the findings from studies on children's development under conditions of adversity conducted over recent decades. The working paper found that **learning to cope with manageable threats to our physical and social well-being is critical for the development of resilience***. It also indicated that positive and negative experiences over time continue to influence a child's mental and physical development, showing that resilience can be built; it's not an innate trait or a resource that can be used up.

*Resilience is measured in terms of how children's brains, immune systems, and genes all respond to stressful experiences. (2015)

SLIPS, SETBACKS AND SUCKING IT UP

"I am not what has happened to me. I am what I choose to become."

— Carl Jung

It seems surreal writing this but nearly 20 years to the day after I became disabled, I felt disabled for the first time. It was a huge smack in the face, (not literally I hasten to add – but it did feel like it). I contracted a virus aged 18 while on a gap year in Australia. It caused catastrophic damage to the nerves in my lower limbs, resulting in loss of function. I guess you could say it was a massive setback to my plans of travelling the world before University. So why didn't I ever really feel disabled? Probably because at 18 you consider yourself invincible. I believed the doctors were wrong and that everything would be okay. I was willing to accept my current situation as I believed it to be temporary. That doesn't, of course, mean there weren't frustrations or bad moments. There were, but what intrigues me is why it took a wrist injury 20 years later to actually feel disabled? What was it about this relatively minor setback that had such a huge impact on my mental health and wellbeing, derailing my life as a high-performance athlete just as I was seeking to sit on the top step of the podium?

I think it was that I hadn't understood the impact of this setback. I hadn't realised how it would impact the things I took for granted. And I just wasn't ready for the challenge it threw at me. The situation in which I found myself left me with a real lack of identity. Who was I, if I couldn't be Emma Wiggs the world-beating canoeist? This is a dangerous place in which to find yourself, but an easy one to fall into. Our jobs take a huge amount of our time and energy. It's easy to find yourself introducing yourself as your job title. And so, if a setback threatens that position in which we hold ourselves, it can be crushing.

No matter how big or small setbacks are on our quest to our performance goal, we can be ready for them. And subsequently (hopefully) suffer less impact by them. Different things can derail us at different times, but seeking to understand our own vulnerabilities will hopefully mean we are a little more prepared for them. Recognising times when we may be lower in energy (or indeed, tolerance) could help reduce flash points that could be damaging to our confidence or our performance going forwards. It allows us to cut ourselves some slack and realise there are times when we can go at a slightly slower pace. Be less demanding of ourselves and others in order to be more productive later on. These moments will be different for everyone, often depending on work targets, time commitments, family calendars and a whole host of things that impact our daily life. For females, even menstrual cycles can impact our performance. Highlighting moments when hormones may impact our energy levels or concentration for tasks could be a huge asset in managing ourselves when setbacks strike.

Remembering you always have a choice is a massively important factor when setbacks hit us. I have a choice in how I respond to this. I have a choice where I go next. I have a choice over how this will define me or impact my performance going forwards. It's an empowering thing to realise. In sport, business or life, things sometimes seem unfair. Reminding yourself that you have chosen to be doing this (and you could equally choose not to) quite often jolts us back to focusing on the task and challenge – rather than the personal feelings we are experiencing.

Forewarned is forearmed in this situation. Without wanting to be a doom-and-gloom advocate, I do believe it is vital that we prepare for setbacks, slips or situations where others' behaviours might be very challenging for us. By thinking about what they may look like and how they may make us feel, we can be prepared and ready. And therefore find that they have less of a negative impact than we might expect. One tactic I've found very helpful is what I call Bullshit Bingo. Think about those situations or people in your daily environment whose behaviours can negatively impact an aspect of your performance, whether it be your own mood, your energy levels, your happiness, your confidence or your focus. If left unchecked these mood-hoovers can suck away at your productivity and, over time, have a detrimental effect on your performance. I had such a situation, where a teammate would choose to try to impact my training in a negative way. A comment here, or an action there. I would let these deliberate acts eat away at my confidence, my focus and most importantly, my energy levels. I would moan and obsess about the impact they were having, rather than taking some simple actions to minimise it. So, I developed Bullshit Bingo. I prepared a sheet with all the negative comments or actions that I had grown so used to. This way when they appeared, as I knew they would, I ticked them off in my mind rather than getting distracted and annoyed at their appearance.

This sounds childish, but it worked. I found myself smiling inside that I had batted off the attempted strike at my focus, energy or confidence, and won the battle, by ticking off another box. Each bingo line or full house came with a little reward and it was hugely satisfying to reach that knowing I had not only deflected it and kept my focus on my performance but strengthened my armour to future attacks. It's all about control, really. Taking challenging situations and finding a way to gain some control when you can't actually stop how some people behave.

Even if we haven't planned for it, when that slip or setback comes we can seek to understand it. Accept it. Process it. And then package it. To help us not only deal with it, but form a plan to move past the current situation. I guess it's about resilience. I had always believed I was quite a resilient person, having gone through the things I had. So I was quite surprised that a wrist injury could derail that and pour doubt on everything. Let's assume resilience is fluid and that we can learn some key strategies in times of setbacks that will fundamentally help us find the path out the other side.

So, when setbacks or slip ups come our way, I would urge us to find the opportunity to seek out something that we can control. While also becoming comfortable with being uncomfortable. Feeling sorry for ourselves for a prolonged period of time will rarely lead us where we want to go. It's okay to feel rubbish and disappointed (and actually it's important to recognise these as it means the task we were pursuing was important to us). However, the sooner we can bounce back to a positive, challenge-embracing mindset, the better. Using past experiences can be very helpful in dealing with new setbacks. Often, we want to forget tough times and move on. But actually, evaluating what helped us overcome them is vitally important. Being able to say to ourselves: 'Okay, I've been here before and I came out the other side' is quite empowering. Think of it as your imaginary buffer. Pull on that protective coat and arm yourself with the things you know will help you.

Most of all, be kind to yourself. Setbacks are part of life and most of us would do well to remember to cut ourselves some slack, take some time and be world class in self-care. Before we reflect, refocus and recharge our energy to tackle the situation at hand. Then, when you're ready, you can pull on your big girl (or boy) pants and head to our pre-planned strategies that we know will help.

Coaching Questions

1. Recover: Make sure when setbacks happen you regroup and evaluate how you recovered. This is vital learning for next time.

2. Bad: What's the worst that can happen? Am I happy to live with potential consequences?

3. Recycle: In the moment of a setback: Have you been here before? Is there anything you learned then that could help now? (Even if it's just 'I've been here before')

4. Reflect: What went well? How would you finish the sentence 'It would be even better if...' Even in a setback, evaluate what went well and what you would do differently.

5. Innovate: Could you have done anything differently?

Habituators

1. Accept: 'When life gives you lemons, make lemonade'. What will your lemonade recipe be?

2. Shift: Has my goal changed? What steps can I start taking now to get back on track.

3. Care: Be world class at self-care. Give yourself what you need now to ensure you are then ready to bounce back.

4. Thanks: What are you grateful for in your life? This is a task that can really help set some perspective and, done periodically, realigns us with our values and what is important.

5. Integrate: Does this setback change who you are? You are more than one result, one set back or one slip-up. Remember the whole person and use these occasions as crucial learning opportunities.

TEAMWORK AND TOGETHERNESS

"On a football team, it's not the strength of its individual players, but it is the strength of the unit and how it all functions together."

— Bill Belichick, *Head Coach, New England Patriots*

Team Me is my secret weapon. Don't tell any of my competitors, but it is the people around me that create the performances and allow someone like me to achieve the things we have. (Trust me, there is nothing special about me.) So, what is it that has meant we have won multiple world titles and broken the world's fastest times over eight years? Within most performance environments, whether it's business or sport, people have the same opportunities, the same access to technology or the same exposure to the staff they work with. So what makes the difference between someone who performs and someone who doesn't make it? Some would say it's an element of luck, but I'm not a fan of that viewpoint. I believe you make your own success, based on the decisions you make in those crucial moments. Including the relationships you form with vital people and the strength of the team you build around you.

Having competed first in a team sport and then an individual one, I'm often asked was it hard to lose the team around you? In fact, I believe I'm part of the greatest team on the planet even though I paddle my boat by myself. An effective team is one which shares a set of common values and works towards an agreed goal for each other. This doesn't mean you can't have your own goals but the higher purpose of the team has to be shared. People may have different ideas of how to achieve the goals set. But by agreeing the way forward, the team becomes stronger as they strive towards the shared goal. The feeling of being part of a team is not for everyone. Some feel they don't need the support of others and can do just fine by themselves. And that's okay, too. However, I feel confident that if you can create a team around you that understands, supports and challenges, you are likely to achieve far greater things than if you trod the road yourself.

And the key to having a powerful, secret-weapon-of-a-team, who will guide you and seek out opportunities to challenge each other and ensure you are all working to the same level? It is all down to everyone agreeing to live by the mantra.

Understand

Seek to first understand the situation, don't jump in and judge or panic. Look for facts.

Support

Offer compassion. It's amazing how a listening ear can help.

Challenge

This is vital. Be prepared to question and challenge, in a positive way, every member of the team. Challenge and be challenged, is how we grow and develop and reach the heights of performance we may have never thought we could reach.

It can be easy to jump straight to challenges when things don't go to plan or when people look like they're not pulling their weight. Trust me, I've done it; challenging why people don't turn up early enough to warm up properly, why someone gives half-effort to a session. These situations rarely play out positively and usually leave me feeling worse than the person involved. However, by seeking to understand why someone might be behaving in a particular way or not living up to the standards they usually do, we can gain an understanding without the confrontational and energy-sapping aspect.

By understanding, we can then support; and allow this process to unfold. We are then able to challenge in a positive way. Whilst always remembering we can only control the controllables, this doesn't mean we can't be empathetic and interested in those we value and work with, to try and get the most out of them and ourselves. I have found it far more effective and rewarding to adopt a role model type approach rather than a confrontational one. Hoping my behaviours and actions help create the environment I believe will benefit everyone.

By living by a shared set of values and behaviours we form greater connections. I've always valued the impact of the team around me. In fact, I happily attribute every great race to them, preferring to feel empowered by the strength of people alongside, helping me; rather than battling my sometimes lacking self-belief. However, I have only recently realised that by forming greater connections with our Team Me we can get more from each other and achieve more than any of us potentially expected. So, what do we mean by connections? It's all about ensuring everyone sees the value in something for them: Why should they help you? Why should they invest energy time and effort in pursuing a goal that is ultimately yours? Well, it's because by having the right conversations that goal becomes everyone's, that quest towards it becomes everyone's desire and you bring them along with you; empowered and engaged, to get the best from everyone. I don't talk about when I won this or I delivered that performance, I talk about 'we'; about how 'we' worked hard, 'we' found a way and 'we' delivered when it mattered.

I truly believe there is nothing special about me, (apart from the incredibly impressive wheelie I can pull in my wheelchair). What is special is the team around me and how we work together. Most athletes have the same opportunity with the same staff. But do they engage and connect in a way that gets that little bit extra out of them, by ensuring they feel valued and part of it? Maybe not. By caring and constantly seeking to understand, support and challenge each other in the right way, we can build a team who are committed, hardworking and driven towards high performance moments. And surely a shared journey travelled together is more successful? As Vince Lombardi once said: 'Individual commitment to a group effort – that is what makes a team work, a company work, a society work, a civilisation work.'

Coaching Questions

1. Coalesce: Are we all on the same page? How do you know?

2. Clarify: Is everyone clear on the end goal, the process to get there and their role?

3. Share: Have you made an effort to express the value others bring to your journey?

4. Master: Have you adopted the Understand, Support, Challenge approach?

5. Expedite: How can you get the best from your team? What makes them tick?

Habituators

1. Discover: Try working on a psychometric analysis of personalities. Understanding each other is a hugely important step in performing together.

2. Chat: Sometimes the small conversations and making connections with people outside of your shared goal build a stronger team.

3. Recognise: Acknowledge input of others.

4. Enquire: Have a questioning approach to everything but allow time for these conversations. Rushed conversations rarely end positively and certainly won't maximise the potential benefits.

5. True: Be honest and authentic when looking at your own performances. Being true to your values and holding your hands up will ensure your team are on board.

Studies from the Center for Neuroeconomics Studies at Claremont Graduate University have shown that **when a person is intentionally trusted, even by a stranger, the brain produces oxytocin, a chemical that reduces the typical wariness of interacting with those we do not know** and increases ability to empathise. The higher the trust, the more oxytocin is released.

ULTIMATE

"Sometimes you win and sometimes you learn."

— John Maxwell

It's nice to win isn't it? It's nice to be a winner and it's nice to have the reinforcement of our successes. It can create feelings of self-belief and give us confidence. It's human nature to celebrate any little wins that life may throw at us. The traffic light that changes to green as we approach. The bonus of just making it into the office before a downpour. The smug feeling of just getting that extra rep in before the countdown clock bleeps. Wins are important but they're not the most important. Sometimes the actual win is completely out of our control and therefore it would be madness to judge ourselves purely on that outcome, wouldn't it? But we do. Too often we have the win, and beating others, as the ultimate measure of success or failure. And this can lead to negative feelings and impact our future performances.

Obviously, the ultimate winning moment will be positive for some whilst negatively impacting others. We have to ask ourselves how this sits with us? Sometimes you don't really know what winning may mean unless you consider what it may feel like to lose? So, is the ultimate win worth it at any cost? How will this make you feel? What impact could the win have on you? The trick is in how we define winning or frame success and how we subsequently harness the power of any win or indeed any failure-to-win. The word 'compete' comes from 17th century Latin word 'competere' meaning 'to strive or compete together' for something. How would it change our thoughts and feelings or indeed our anxiety in the important moments if we reframed winning and competing as 'striving together' for something? I would argue this has huge potential for athletes and non-athletes alike. If we viewed our competitors as equals, striving with us and pushing us towards our goal, rather than someone who is against us, it could lead to less stress every day. And a more relaxed environment where we can truly reach our potential, uninhibited by worries or anxiety.

Sometimes winning is out of our control. We could have trained hard, practiced over and over and delivered our absolute best in the moment but someone else just delivers the unexpected performance of their lives and beats us. Completely out of our control. We could feel robbed of the ultimate win but if we have been clever and defined what success looks like to us then even in defeat there is a win and a huge learning opportunity. By reassessing how we measure success we can actually steer ourselves to more wins. More relevant successes. More impactful performances. Potentially beyond any expectations we may have originally had.

Winning, by nature, happens to the few. Whatever the situation or challenge, there can usually only be one winner, therefore creating many more losers. Is the seeking of this singular moment (and multiple subsequent damages to others) really going to make us feel like we've achieved the ultimate? Should we be chasing the ultimate win or should we be cleverer and more calculated to ensure daily wins, which possibly have more positive and enduring impact on ourselves and our performances? As an athlete, the answer is not quite as simple as you may think. Do I only chase gold medals? Is my sole goal to win gold medals by paddling a piece of fiberglass faster than anyone else down a 200m course? Is my ultimate win based on others being losers? Of course, to be on the top step of a podium with a shiny piece of metal around your neck is, I guess, an ultimate moment. But is it the ultimate win? Probably not. In fact, I clearly remember being on that top step in Rio 2016 and being disappointed with the time that had just beaten the rest of the world and won me the race. I'd felt flustered by weather conditions pre-race and abandoned my warm up. In fact my own coach gave me a 7/10 for my performance – so how could this be the ultimate win?

If I had considered my golden moment in the Rio Paralympics as my ultimate-ultimate, would I have come home, worked harder than ever in training to identify new small wins to make the boat go faster? And would we have beaten the world record the following year, winning the first ever grand slam of titles in paracanoe in the process? Reframing our measurement of success and looking closely at how and where we attribute that success should mean a continuation of our desire and drive to keep going in search of that truly ultimate win. For me, medals won't define me. In the same way that losing my first international race doesn't change who I am. The ultimate win is making the boats as fast as I possibly can, by working hard. Living by my values. Helping those I care about. If medals come along the way, then even better. But, as I've proved, even that top of the world winning gold moment might not actually be your ultimate win. So keep seeking, keep reassessing what your win looks like for you.

Coaching Questions

1. Define: What does success look like? (Be very clear on this)

2. Specify: What will the win take?

3. Think: Work out what you're grateful for. Will these things change depending on the outcome of the result you seek?

4. Determine: What level of effort will deliver a payoff?

5. Evaluate: How will you evaluate the win: along the way and at the end?

Habituators

1. Small: Are there any small wins you can make starting now?

2. Imagine: Spend some time looking at some scenarios. What will you do in these moments? (What ifs?)

3. Fuel: What are your superpowers and what is your kryptonite?

4. Overcome: How can you mitigate for your kryptonite? (e.g. hangry: stash of snacks)

5. Edge it: Is there anything you can do that will give you the edge? These small acts can fuel our belief and confidence for when we reach those performance moments.

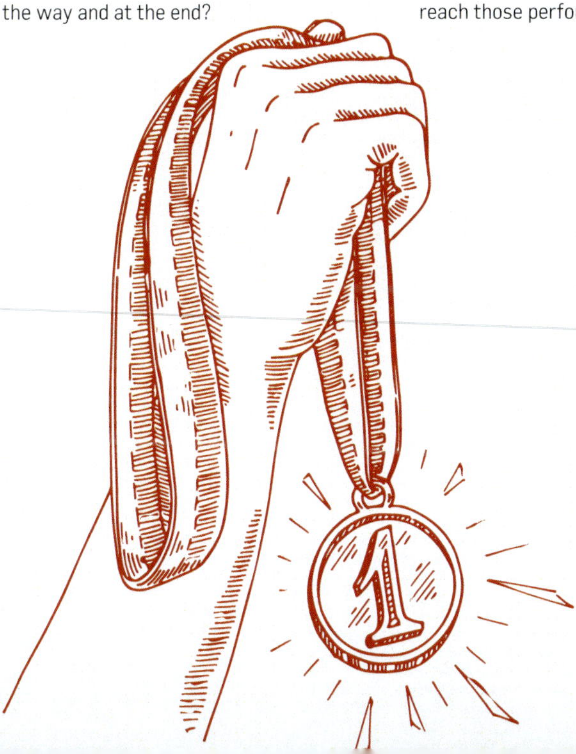

VALUES

"Values are like fingerprints.
Nobody's are the same,
but you leave 'em all over
everything you do."

— Elvis Presley

Values stand at the very core of human decision making. Our values will inform our thoughts, our words and our actions. I'm sure we can all think of a situation where the values we hold dear have influenced our actions and behaviours. This might have been helpful for performance and the outcome we seek, or hinder it. Understanding our values and how they impact our behaviour is a crucial step in making tweaks that will ensure we are in a better position to hit those performance highs.
Values are deeply held principles, ideals, or beliefs that we refer to when making decisions.
Our behaviours often reflect our values but similarly, we can use them to check and challenge ourselves when we may not be living as closely as we might think to the things that are important to us. My values are key to the behaviours I demonstrate at times that can be potentially limiting to my performance. Working out your own values is a hugely important step in any performance pathway – or indeed, journey to living your life well. Spending some time reflecting on what drives the decisions I make, and the behaviours I was showing, was a crucial next step in my performance journey.
It's not a particularly comfortable exercise. It requires honesty and reflection and an open mind. But it absolutely will mean I can unlock some hidden potential, and possibly, energy to use in my pursuit to high performance.

I certainly went through at least 35 years of my life not properly understanding my values and the importance these play on both my performance and my happiness. Ultimately, we've all heard the saying, 'A happy athlete/worker is a successful one.' So why are so many

of us unable to quickly and accurately list our set of values? Well, probably because we haven't ever really sat down and worked them out.
Working with a sports psychologist and finally putting pen to paper on my values was so enlightening. It took some tweaking and refining but eventually left me with four distinct values that shape the person I am. We then looked at identifying behaviours that would demonstrate these values. After all, if these are the things that make me me, I want to know what behaviours demonstrate them. Subsequently, this also highlighted behaviours that are not true to my values and therefore ones that I could try to limit or control day to day. The ones we know are unhelpful, but that usually raise their heads in times of stress, conflict or challenge. I was shocked at the results. By simply being aware, the undesirable behaviours reduced and the positive ones increased. I took great comfort in knowing my values and better understood my sometimes-passionate response to things. The final step was to share these with those I work closely with. For example, my value about being independently-dependable is crucial for my coach to understand to allow us to work effectively together. I don't want to feel that people have to do things for me, rather that I am an important part of the team. And that my contributions help negate the need for occasional help carrying my boat or whatever it may be.

The process of sharing my values with the team around me is the next hugely important step. Explaining to people why I may have lots of questions. Why, at times, I may feel inadequate and not good enough. (Because of my perfectionist tendencies and my deep-rooted values of always doing my best.) This helps create an understanding, so that these behaviours aren't seen negatively, but just as part of me; which is less stressful for both me and them. We can then agree on a set of behaviours that we are all accountable for. In my example, we recognise that my need to question sometimes led to people feeling defensive and this stifled positive performance conversations. We agreed that I would use a shared live document to log questions and allow others time to answer or indeed time for me to reassess the importance of the inquisition I had initiated. This created an agreed culture, based on a set of shared values, which in turn has driven positive performance habits. These habits will drive performance-focused behaviours and these behaviours will in turn drive results. Simple really; culture drives habits, habits drive behaviours and behaviours drive results.

Overall our values are within us and can probably not be changed. However the behaviours that we exhibit as a result of these most definitely can be. Understanding your Why is crucial to revealing your values. Why do we do what we do? Why does it matter to us? What motivates us, what is important to us? All questions that will help us understand our values. Then we have to identify behaviours that demonstrate our values and also, and possibly more importantly, behaviours that do not. This gives us a ready-made list of dos and don'ts from which to work as we try to shape more positive performance behaviours. Aligning our behaviours and performance to our values will also increase our happiness and contentment. If I'm living by the values that are important to Emma Wiggs every day, the outcome of a 48-second canoe race should a) take care of itself, but more importantly, b) not change Emma Wiggs the person.

Coaching Questions

1. **Purpose:** What's your Why?

2. **Values:** Work out your main four or five values.

3. **Action:** What behaviours demonstrate your values?

4. **Reverse:** What behaviours do not demonstrate your values?

5. **Adjust:** Can you make any tweaks to these behaviours?

Habituators

1. **Remember:** Remind yourself of your values every morning.

2. **Select:** Choose an attitude while you brush your teeth every morning that will demonstrate you living by your values as you tackle the day ahead.

3. **Reflect:** Check in at night time with how you did today at showing behaviours that underpin your values.

4. **Plan:** Be prepared for tough days by having a plan ready for challenging moments.

5. **Filter:** Develop a 'Bullshit Bingo' sheet to help you stay on track.

Researchers at UCLA discovered that **reflecting on personal values can actually lower your stress response, and keep it that way.** The study conducted by Dr. Ryan Niemiec showed that those who thought about their highest values before a stressful event actually experience less stress and show a substantial decrease in the stress hormone cortisol, compared to control groups.

WHO IS WHO?

"Be yourself, everyone else is taken."

— Oscar Wilde

We live in a social context. What defines us? In my life I've been a barman, toilet cleaner, paper boy. Are these things who I am? I did learn lots from each job. But they are not me. I was talking with a very senior consultant in a global company recently and they said: 'I'd like to move on from my job being my life.' What we do doesn't define who we are. When we began writing this book we spent some time asking ourselves: Who are we really?

Society puts lots of pressures on us and other people have a great deal of expectation. Sometimes we put that pressure on ourselves. What people think of us and the labels they use, can if we choose, become part of who we are. But it's also true that it doesn't define who we are. In our conversations whilst writing this book, Emma said she didn't want to be defined by medals or disability. Steve said he didn't want to be defined by his military experience and I didn't want to be defined by the label of entrepreneur. I also don't like being labeled as a boss as I find it removes some of my personhood. How can it be, that talented (another label?) people don't want to be defined by things that others aspire to?

We jointly recognise that we prefer being seen as people. I think we all also know the fragility of defining ourselves through status or other perishable means. We open a door to being crushed when these things fade, disappear or are threatened. In the same way that sometimes our bank card is declined, so we too can decline the labelling by others. And in doing so we are then choosing for ourselves what we want. I'd much rather be known to be fun, optimistic, creative and responsible. I don't need the status tag. I don't need the success label. I'd rather dodge that bullet and instead focus on my own excellence, performance and balance. Labels are a distraction, and they also peg us to our past, rather than our future. Even at 42, I still want to live in the moment, and be open to the possibilities of who I will become, rather than what I've done. I asked Emma to share a little on what defines her. She said:

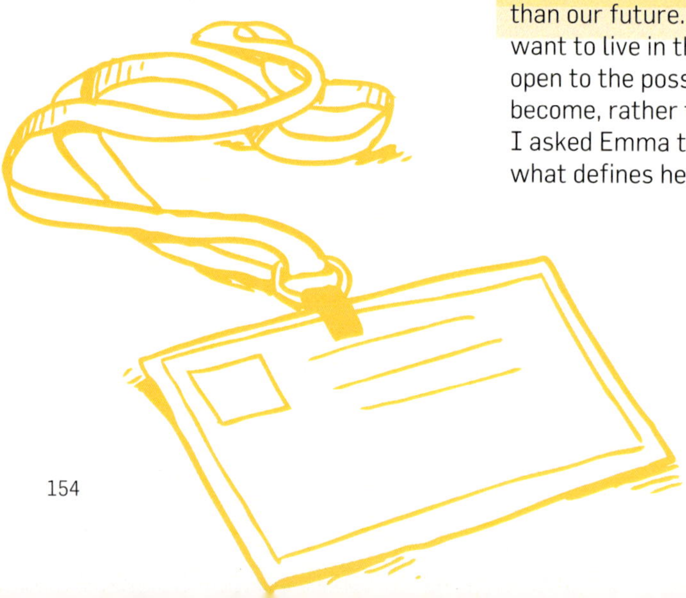

'The word 'define' implies boundaries or limits that we may have, which to me seems crazy. I'm 39 and still finding new limits in some things that I can do, higher and lower. Yet, in work interviews or conversations we are always asked to define ourselves. I'm keen to show that it is our attitudes and behaviours that define us, not so much our abilities. It is our choices at key moments and day to day – e.g. accepting or avoiding challenge – that define how well we do or how happy we are. I would like to think my values define me. My passion. My determination. My integrity. And my ability to be dependable but also vulnerable. Values can feel fluid and changeable at times, but if I always hold them true and understand them, they should really be the true definition of me.'

To perform consistently at a high level is easier with a clear mind and self-acceptance. Other people also find it easiest to be around us when we are uncomplicated, open, kind. Within all of us there can be a battle between our best self and our worst self. Some people call the worst self our shadow, the part of us that can be mean, unkind, selfish, over-competitive. Understanding our shadow and learning to change our relationship with those parts of ourselves is another fruitful adventure on our journey to being the best we can be. Part of what is challenging about living an authentic life is we give up some of the protection and control that keeps us safe from situations and other people. Yet at the same time this transparency can unleash extremely high levels of energy. When we are playing the role, deep down we know it's not really us. It's a sham. A facade. That can consume energy. Somehow as we can become childlike in our self-acceptance life gets easier. In my coaching work I'm always asking: 'What's the [insert name here] way of doing this?' What's your way? When we live life on our own terms and do things the way we believe they should be done, we will have no regrets, even if we fail. Yet, when we try to live life as others would have us do it, then if we succeed, it's just because we followed someone else's pattern. And if we fail, we didn't even do it the way we thought best. That's a lose-lose.

The paradox is that authenticity sounds brilliant and noble, but can actually mean more of our real thoughts, feelings and emotions spill out into the public arena. Anger, frustration, sadness. Anything we don't like is out there. Here we can take ownership, naming, claiming and then taming these aspects of our characters and working hard. To be better.

Coaching Questions

1. **Identify:** What defines you?

2. **Strengths:** What are your best qualities?

3. **Glow:** How can you make your best qualities shine?

4. **Admit:** What are the shadow parts of your personality? (See if you can identify them all).

5. **Check:** Who places the most expectation on you and how can you change your relationship to those expectations?

Habituators

1. **List:** Write a list of the things that make you *you*. What are the very best bits?

2. **Transparent:** Practice sharing your true emotions in words (e.g. saying them, rather than demonstrating them).

3. **Locate:** Find a mentor or coach who you believe to be really authentic and to know themselves very well.

4. **Diagnose:** As you are browsing media, notice the difference between the truly authentic and those who revert to soundbites and cliché.

5. **Experiment:** Do something out of character. A different restaurant. An unusual genre of film. Notice the contrast.

XENACIOUS

"Here's to the crazy ones.
The misfits. The rebels.
The troublemakers.

The round pegs in the square holes. The ones who see things differently. They're not fond of rules. And they have no respect for the status quo. You can quote them, disagree with them, glorify or vilify them. About the only thing you can't do is ignore them. Because they change things. They push the human race forward. And while some may see them as the crazy ones, we see genius. Because the people who are crazy enough to think they can change the world, are the ones who do."

— Rob Siltanen

Steve Jobs was not the mastermind behind the iconic Apple advert slogan 'Here's to the crazy ones'. Whilst the exact creative process is debated, this seminal text came to life through a collaboration between Apple and its ad agency; led by Rob Siltanen. So, let's give him the plaudits. Pursuing being the best, high performance, the elite can often feel that the right method is eliminating all distraction, following established processes, and using discipline to force ourselves and others to achieve results. We know for sure that the science behind both goal attainment and high performance does require detail-focused process, following both in training and execution. So where does that leave craziness, exploration, creativity, wild times, and the opportunity to explore? What do we do if we feel xenacious (having a yearning for change)?

Malcom Gladwell's book *Outliers* is full of stories of people who have had astonishing success, and dug into some of the strange reasons that they have been successful, unrelated to talent. Yet there are another group of people who have had uncanny success by doing things differently. The film The Flying Scotsman shares the true story of Graeme Obree and his bike 'Old Faithful' built with parts of a washing machine. His craziness led to him breaking the world hour record despite the opposition of the establishment.

A life of focus and discipline can be great in achieving high performance. Yet it can also lead us to feeling unfulfilled, boxed in to our own rhythms and rituals, and ultimately, to a place of staleness and fatigue. Working with top executives in global companies as a coach often provokes dialogue about feeling unfulfilled, bored, and yet, paralysed and scared to do something even a little bit crazy. But when we really dig into what makes an amazing life story it is these moments of madness that define us, and can prove a key turning point, that in hindsight was massive.

High performers tend not to run on impulse. Sadly, you can't always plan a little craziness or spontaneity. The ubiquitous pivot made famous by tech entrepreneurs can look like wisdom in hindsight. But nobody really wanted the failures that caused the pivot in the first place.

Human beings are truly creative creatures. We can have wild ideas, flights of fancy, visions, hallucinations. We can tap into our imagination, innovate. We have the ability to create alchemy by mixing ideas. We can even sometimes manifest success through visualisation or other esoteric techniques.

So, when's a good time to try something new? And when is maverick experimentation a disaster?

Our research categorises three situations where craziness might occur, but only two where it's useful, and one where it's essential. Working out which moment we are in is the key to knowing when to unlock our crazy and when to reign it in.

Big Moments

For those interested in high performance, big moments are absolutely not the time to try something new and crazy. Stick to boring. Stick to the known. However tempting, big moments are the time for tried-and-tested, well-established efforts, using pre-existing and well-honed skills. Don't change your diet just before a big race, or (as I did once) don't try a new keynote style for one of your biggest ever gigs. Just don't. (Sorry, Paul.) Despite the lure of a switch-up for that extra 10%, it's not the time. Stick to what you know.

Cliff Hangers

These feel similar to Big Moments. There's lots at stake, it's a crucial time, the pressures on, but the situation has got so bad doing something, anything is better than doing nothing. Startups often get to this situation, where everything we have tried is not working, and we have to try something else, anything else. We have nothing to lose by trying but it is also the case that if we don't try something crazy it's all lost anyway.

No Downsides

In these moments, experimentation should be easy. Moments where there are no downsides to giving something new ago. Sometimes in poker there are no-downsides moments for a big bet, even going all-in. Generally, these are when you hold a great hand. Even more so if you hold "the nuts" (the best hand possible). Athletes may try some new training methods after a successful Olympic games. Business leaders may invest in innovation off the back of a season of great profits. Maybe it's just taking the family on a different kind of holiday. Some seasons of life are just a good time to get wild and creative in a low-risk and truly free way.

Coaching Questions

1. Party: What are your quirks and weird bits? How can you celebrate them more?

2. Grow: What aspects of your crazy side could you amplify and what might happen if you tap into it more?

3. Visualise: What are your up-and-coming big moments?

4. Build: How can you build the bravery to just go for it in the cliff hangers that are to come in life?

5. Distil: Have a careful think across the aspects of your life. Where are the hidden, no-downsides opportunities currently lying untapped?

Habituators

1. Master: Take something to mastery. A hobby, a work skill. When we have done our 10,000 hours, our frame of reference changes.

2. Explore: Read a book about a wild risk-taker. Poker books. World Travel. War. Sport. What can you learn about the approach to the new, wild and unknown?

3. Embrace: Experiment with 'yes' over 'no'.

4. Increase: Expand your circle. Who do you know that is a good role model for the right kind of risk-taking? Ask them if you can interview them for a blog.

5. Imagine: Write a list of adventures you would like to undertake in the next few months.

A study by the International Journal of Environmental Research and Public Health evaluated 21 relevant papers to assess the effects of risky outdoor play (including great heights, high speed and risk of getting lost) on children's health. It indicated that **risky play supportive environments increased play time, physical activity and behaviours such as social interactions, creativity and resilience**, and decreased acute sedentary behaviours.

Y

YARNS

"So, Matilda's strong young mind continued to grow, nurtured by the voices of all those authors who had sent their books out into the world like ships on the sea. These books gave Matilda a hopeful and comforting message: You are not alone."

— Roald Dahl, *Matilda*

Stories are what sets Homo sapiens apart from the rest of the animal kingdom. We all have a story. A past. A future ahead. There have been twists and turns for all of us. PR gurus and politicians are obsessed with being in control of the narrative. What's the relevance of yarns in understanding high performance?

Funnily enough, stories are a key ingredient. Our brains are full of stories. Telling yarns and tales is how we make sense of the world. It's how others get to know us. To join in with us or oppose us. We are a story, but what character are we? Hero? Villain? Victim? Supporting cast? Who are we in other people's story? When coaching, I often ask leaders to consider:

- Are we creating the life story we want?
- When we look back, what's the story we want to tell?
- What stories are we collecting and sharing? A good life involves escapades and a rich tapestry of experiences.
- How does this chapter of our current story end?
- How can we improve as a storyteller?

In my role as a CEO I have to tell stories to my staff. In my role as a sales person I have to use stories to influence customers.

In my role as a father I create stories and story experiences to enrich the lives of my kids and prompt (I hope), some elements of wonder. Stories provoke emotion, and are easily stored in memory, transported, and can be shared and spread like wild fire. In his excellent book '*The Seven Basic Plots: Why We Tell Stories*' Christopher Booker argues there are seven archetypes that almost all stories conform to. We can use these to intentionally shape stories in two ways. Firstly, we can consider the story we are telling ourselves about our own lives. And secondly, we can use these structures to shape up stories we want to use to tell others.

1. Overcoming the Monster

There is an evil force threatening our hero, their world, mankind. This is the story of high performing campaigners like Greta Thunberg, and other purpose-driven campaigners.

2. Rags to Riches

This one is fairly self-explanatory. At the beginning, our hero is insignificant and dismissed by others, but something happens to elevate him, revealing him to be exceptional. This is a very common theme with elite athletes, business people and is often a deep part of the motivation of high performers. Lewis Hamilton is one of the world's most famous examples of this archetype.

3. The Quest

A hero must set out on a long, hazardous journey, and will battle all obstacles until they are triumphant. We see this story often with innovators, entrepreneurs and creatives. It is also the inner journey of many people in politics.

4. Voyage and Return

While also based on a journey, the Voyage and Return is very different from The Quest. Here, the hero travels out of their normal world into the overwhelming and unknown, before escaping back to the safety of their home. The military rhythm of campaigns, or adventurer and explorers are living for this narrative.

5. Comedy

A story made up of comedic events, normally involving mistaken identity, misunderstanding or confusion, resulting in hilarious chaos. Some of us want our life to be a tapestry of hilarious events, or sometimes we experience an episode in our lives that can only be explained as a comedy. Few people set out to live a hilarious life, though many high performing YouTubers are aiming to achieve just this.

6. Tragedy

This is the story without the happy ending. While our other archetypes have seen triumphant heroes and slain monsters, this plot takes a different turn, and ends in loss. Tragedy is all around us in life, and the story of tragedy can be harnessed positively to consider fully our life position and count our blessings. It's also worth noting that all stories can end in tragedy. High performers tend to face this directly and be open that they may ultimately fail, yet not let failure define them.

7. Rebirth

Rebirth stories sees our hero 'alling under a dark spell – whether this is sleep, sickness or enchantment – before breaking free and being redeemed. We all have rebirth stories. And sometimes we must trigger a rebirth in ourselves and others to move on from a challenging phase.

To become influential in our field requires not just results. It requires us to take hold of telling the story. To take ownership of the story. To carefully shape the story. To think about the tone of voice of our stories and the emotions we want to convey. We might think about our favourite storyteller's voice. Does it make us feel excited, sad, fearful, or happy? We may tend to overelaborate and use our amazingly creative mind to make the stories more interesting than perhaps they actually were (if they were/are real). It's valuable to steer the right course and ensure true stories don't become tall stories. Tall storytellers might, for example, tell all team members they are 'the best'. And in doing so, eventually lose credibility. To be respected requires authenticity and truthfulness. We must not become fake news.

Under pressure our brains may attempt to provide unhelpful endings to the story we are in. What if I go bankrupt? What if I don't win the deal? What if I don't win the race? What if my boss doesn't like me? We can become anxious about the future and what story might unfold. We may be anxious, or stressed. Catastrophic fantasy occurs and we start to imagine a chain of terrible events.

High performers tend to take control of these inner stories to avoid unnecessary worry, and wasted energy. They work hard to manage their mind and take control for their emotions. They provide their subconscious with positive endings to the worrying story. Externalising (sharing) our deepest fears to trusted advisor can allow them to provide appropriate perspective and guidance. Basing our inner story on facts helps us save energy and redirect it positively.

Ultimately stories also motivate and inspire; dream, believe, achieve. Yet in the end, it's our own choices and actions that are the actual power in both the story we are in and the story we are creating.

Coaching Questions

1. Narrate: What is the story you tell yourself about your life?

2. Celebrate: What is inspirational about your life story so far?

3. Uncover: What is the story you are telling yourself about how the rest of your life will be?

4. Create: How can you use your imagination to build the future you want?

5. Select: Who are the important characters in your story and how can you involve them in your unfolding narrative?

Habituators

1. Craft: Story telling is a real art. Listen out for those around you who are capable story tellers. How do they craft their story to make it fascinating?

2. Sketch: Do some creative writing about an episode in your life. Write about 500 words. Give the story some shape.

3. Imagine: What do you want for each decade of your life? Start at age 80-90. What life do you want to live then? Work backwards to your current decade. What has to happen now to build the story you want?

4. Select: Identify people it would be valuable for you to influence. Kids, team members, prospective clients. What's the narrative that will move them emotionally to take the actions you want?

5. Purchase: Read something new.

ZZZS

"Your future depends on your dreams, so go to sleep."

— Mesut Barazany

We're nearly there. Stick with us for this last chapter. Then, please, by all means, go to sleep. If you do then we will have hopefully and collectively achieved our aim; to leave you inspired and ready to rest, recover and process all that you've learned in this book so that you can be better prepared for tomorrow (and the bright and exciting future ahead of you).

I read somewhere that humans have a default setting of slight anxiety (perhaps more so today than our ancestors). Thousands of years ago, people were rightly afraid of the dark. They didn't know what dangerous animals were out there (including other groups of humans), they were perhaps unsure as to where breakfast was coming from and they were perhaps cold because their stock of kindling was depleted or wet. Sometimes they may have had good reason to worry and to keep them safe, cortisol (that clever little stress hormone) kept them alive by nagging them to remain vigilant and a little nervous or scared. Maybe this condition was worse in winter because they were wetter and colder than usual, the nights were longer and their favourite berries weren't that abundant. Perhaps it was the prequel to modern day Seasonal Adjustment Disorder (SAD). Cortisol is responsible for waking us in the morning when the melatonin (the natural hormone that helps control the human sleep cycle) levels drop. But annoyingly it also keeps us awake at night when we worry about those things, things that can probably wait until the morning.

Considering that much of my previous work was conducted at night, it may sound strange when I suggest that, if at all possible, leave making any important decisions until the next day. Nowadays, I work with many people that are struggling to come to terms with current or past experiences, or indeed worrying about how to prepare for what's to come.

My advice would be to spend conscious time reflecting on things in the day and let the subconscious processing do its magic at night during some good, well-planned sleep.

In terms of performance, if we don't sleep then we will struggle. At the very least, our performance is adversely affected. At worst, we will die! When tired, we don't make good decisions, we aren't kind, we can be bad friends and we get extremely irritable. Sleep is the best method of recovery, bar none. These days, and with the advances in neuroscience, having no sleep is no longer seen as a 'badge of honour' certainly in high performance settings. To be the best we can be in business, sport, the military, frontline emergency service, law, social care, teaching or at home; we need to sleep (and to sleep well), so I think it's worth getting good at it.

My friend and colleague, Professor Andy McCann, says that sleep is the best legal performance-enhancing activity you can do. In an age where we all seem to lead increasingly busy lives, if we want to up our game, it's certainly worth investing our time and effort in. Even during COVID-19 lockdown, the worries around money and employment, social connection and home-schooling seem to keep us preoccupied and awake. So, when trying to sleep, if something is bothering you or keeping you from sleeping, then try and put the thought aside (sometimes easier said than done, I know), and focus on some good old diaphragmatic (deep) breathing, for instance, and pledge to address the issue when the sun comes up. If you can't sleep after 20-30 minutes of trying then perhaps get up and do something boring for a while (perhaps read my chapters of this book) before trying to sleep again.

The subject of sleep deserves far more space than this chapter can offer but there are some great books out there on sleep as well as some wonderful TED Talks and YouTube clips.

Here are some useful facts and information as well a number of strategies that over the years have helped me sleep better, even in the most uncomfortable settings and scenarios:

- Humans sleep in cycles of roughly 90 minutes. 5 x 90 min cycles = 7.5 hours sleep which is about right for most people per night.
- Short naps of 20-30 minutes in the day are okay to keep us going when times are tough (try not to exceed half an hour as we will start to enter deep sleep when our body literally shuts down for repair and rebuild).
- A perfect scenario would see us sleeping for 35 cycles per week but 25+ is good. Try not to get below 20 sleep cycles per week. This is a useful way to keep track of how much quality sleep (90 min cycle) we're getting, especially if our sleeping pattern is erratic; with shift work, for instance.
- We should aim to wake/get up at roughly the same time each day if our lifestyles/shift patterns allow.
- If we want to squeeze more cycles of sleep in, go to bed earlier, rather than get up later.
- If we are struggling with sleep, try to avoid stimulants, such as caffeine, after lunchtime.
- Prepare for sleep. Bedrooms should be for sleep and sex only. Eject as many electronic devices as necessary!
- We must try not to eat a heavy meal within two hours of going to bed to sleep.
- Alcohol negatively affects quality of sleep. We may feel that we've slept well but alcohol, as with a big meal, puts our body into a stressed state while it processes the alcohol – this impacts our bodies ability to process the day's activities and repair.
- If you currently sleep well, carry on doing what you're doing.

Matt Walker is a world-renowned sleep expert and suggests:

'Sleep is your superpower.... wonderfully good things can happen when you get sleep, but alarmingly bad things happen when you don't get enough, both for your brain and for your body.'

Let's face it we could all do with a superpower, couldn't we? This one is a dead cert, completely within our control. It may require some effort to establish a new routine but ultimately it is something we can all have (and the same cannot be said for flying or invisibility). So why wouldn't we try to maximise it and reap the rewards?

As an athlete, Emma knows all about the importance of sleep. Here's what she's learnt:

'I run on only four hours sleep a night.' 'I've not had breakfast, no time, I'm always first into the office.' 'I send emails late at night, it shows the bosses I'm committed.' 'I skip breakfast and lunch, too busy.' These are all things people in business have said to me over the years. They were keen to tell me how little sleep they have, how dedicated they are by skipping meals or not drinking water. As an athlete I'm all about being competitive but this seemed ridiculous, why would they knowingly set themselves up to perform badly, increase their risk of developing serious health conditions and ensure, by their actions, they may never actually reach their performance potential not to mention potentially not be a happy or content as they could?

I do sympathise with the experiences I mentioned above. At times I've found it hard to rest and recover, choosing to always do more, to gain some ill-judged advantage on competitors from punishing myself and showing off how much I can do. Look at social media; it's rife with competitive posts, whether it be how perfect our lives are or how hard we are working. It's human nature. We should recognise this but also seek to address simple, quick fixes that will actually allow us to reap the rewards of the work we do get done, whilst preparing us to go again the next day. It was a revelation in my training and progress when I started getting enough sleep and recovery to actually realise the hard work I was doing in the gym and on the water. And remember, recovery doesn't have to be sleep. Purely being horizontal, relaxing, reading, allowing mind and body to recover and prepare for good sleep is just as important. Altering my bedtime was one of the most impactful changes I made.'

Advice

1. Set same bedtime and wake time whether it's a weekday or the weekend. Bedroom temperature of around 65 degrees (18 degrees Celsius).
2. Have a routine and stick to it.
3. Change your mindset. Imagine how impressed people would be if you were as good as you are and got eight hours sleep a night. Try that for a badge of honour.

Coaching Questions

1. Query: Do I have sleep problem? Using a scale of 1-10, how would I assess my sleep?

2. Pick: What one small thing can I do to improve my chances of getting better sleep?

3. Admit: What issues regularly keep me awake at night?

4. Count: How many sleep cycles have I achieved in the past seven days (25-35 sleep cycles are what we should be aiming for 20 or less is cause for concern).

5. Learn: Do I need to educate my sleeping partner on the science of sleep?

The Philips 2020 Global Sleep Survey surveyed more than 13,000 adults across 13 countries to capture sleep attitudes, perceptions and behaviours. The survey indicated that **whilst 51% of adults are not satisfied with their sleep, only 10% have sought help from a sleep specialist.**

Habituators

1. Clock it: Set a time that you want to be up and awake by, and then work backwards to the time when you need to be asleep. If you would like 7.5 hours sleep and you need to be awake at 7am then you ideally need to be asleep by 11.30pm. Try and give yourself around 15 mins to get to sleep, so you should be getting into bed around 11.15pm. If you feel you need nine hours' sleep then you need to be sleeping by 10pm.

2. Switch: Do vigorous exercise earlier in the day, less exertive exercise later on.

3. Scribble: We often find ourselves worrying about things when we get to bed as our mind starts to unwind. Either put a pen and paper next to your bed so that you can transfer thoughts or better still, spend a moment before bed (out of the bedroom) emptying your head of things that may prevent you from sleep.

4. Relax: Deep rhythmic breathing helps you get to sleep.

5. Prioritise: Remember that sleep is the best form of recovery we have, so if required don't worry about it, make necessary changes and invest in sleep.

FINAL THOUGHTS

So, what? Why is all this important? Why should we invest time and effort into performing better?

Integration into your life is key. We are all different, and we'll all have differing takes on what we've just read. Key to this making a difference to you is how you adapt it; to your story, your experience, your journey. There will undoubtedly be highs and lows in times to come. But how you face them will dictate your happiness and wellbeing.

Knowing that, you can do several things; starting with doing nothing and looking forward to the unexpected or you can approach it with a degree of wisdom (which you hope to build on) and have your mind open and your metaphorical toolbox at the ready to face life front-on. Disappointments and setbacks will be aplenty but when you get flattened by an event that rocked your world, what will you need to get back up? Who will you need around you? And what will you want to say to yourself when you're back at it?

FINALLY: WORDS

Hope you enjoyed that. Food for thought. Fuel for the fire. Or hopefully as the Dutch say, a Golden Egg Moment. Twenty-six thoughts are far too many to remember. The joy of an alphabet book though is that we can make some words. Perhaps that's a way to anchor some thoughts for a season.

Feeling stressed?
How about RAT? Responsibility, Resilience and the Rough Stuff, Attitude, plus Teamwork and Togetherness.

Want to perform?
Maybe it's BIG! Beliefs, Ikigai, Goals and Growth.

Need to clear your mind?
Maybe you need some special FX?
Flexibility, Freedom and Fun, plus a little craziness with Xenacious and Xany.

Pick a few letters.
Make a new phrase.
It doesn't have to be grammatically correct.

Innovate a whole new process: PNQ could be the way to remember to:

1. Make a proper Plan,
2. Say No to a few Noises, and
3. Ask some Quality Questions.

Whatever we choose to take forward there are plenty of ways to integrate simple concepts used by those who strive for the highest levels of performance, and integrate them into our repertoire for life. Tried and tested. Across multiple disciplines.

Our bit is done.
The rest is over to you.

More books published by Interactive Workshops
Available on Amazon

THE AGILE SECRET

How is it that certain people are able to drive results and be responsive to change? Can be firm, yet open? People-people and task-people? What's their secret? It's simple.They are deploying agile strategies.

Agile is the fastest and best way to get stuff done. That's a fact. And agile can work for anybody. So, dive into this book if you want to:

- Improve speed and efficiency to get work done
- Supercharge the way teams work collaboratively
- Become a leader that creates dynamic, productive, adaptable, self-motivated and self-organising teams

All it takes is a slim amount of knowledge, some belief and a pinch of bravery. That's enough to lead a revolution.

TEAM BY TEAM

Learn to create true belonging and get massive results. Working in teams is part of what it means to work. Team by Team is packed with over 100 brilliant ideas about how to get the most from yourself and the people around you. And it's the only team building book actually written by a team.

Read this book if you want to:

- Feel more connected to co-workers and be more real at work
- Lead a team that performs to a high level and is genuinely great fun to be part of
- Belong to something that is more than just a job
- Improve results
- Build working relationships that can last a lifetime